POEMS : 1988

BY

BRENDAN TRIPP

POEMS : 1988

ISBN 978-1-57353-017-0

ESCHATON™

http://www.EschatonBooks.com

1988

JANUARY 1988

ON JOURNEYS NEWLY MADE

rails extend through time
the "el" carries me north
abstraction becomes
all the earth
a world of views
extracted, vague
set in some haze
within the mind

familiar sights are taken by
I ride alone through minor crowds
the words
are not sufficient
memory does not allow
the flowering of night
caught in image
in crystal set

places long ago are cut
by movement in this present light
almost expecting
faces lost
to make return in this
I lose their names
I lose my own
to this decay of life

the sun bleeds westward, draining day
as appointments call the northward flow
bits fly by
kaleidoscopic
the tide now cycles
ever inward
making up a change of life
tearing at the poisoned soul

termination heralds its approach
with visions of eternal trials
cards are dealt
against the dark
allotting facts
and places to the eye
so like the final blade
dividing will from flesh

- Brendan Tripp
01/02/1988

STRUCK BY DELIMITATION

stress is time's equal
made ragged in regard
to the open range
not offered to the mob
eliminated by desire
filed against the faulty grid

so descends
months hard at the drawing air
which twists bands tightly
in destruction of the mind

knowledge comes slowly
if at all
and words become too weak to bear
the load of concept asked of them
too many books flood days
and more demand their share
focus rips
unable to withstand the strain
of angularity in variance
and so creates a void

it wonders if
chemicals intrude
and wash away the clearer point
the world swirls by
without a vantage held
to give a meaning
definitions to divine

massive duplication strikes
too great to hide
cloaked but by darkness
and alternates of absence made
strained limitless
given sway within the night
too much a making to fall complete
against this leaving's length

- Brendan Tripp
01/03/1988

BROKEN WISHES CAUGHT IN

fiction
     allowed
this seems
                    alien
have not the effort
TIME
     because   of
chain chain chain chain chain
the same old
     story
the same old
               pain
hours are
parties
     are
     wasted
depression's day is on the rise
whip with steel tipped
          lashes
bleed and bleed and bleed
     no good there
          no good here
into darkness
     death
               despair
wells from deep within
making
     a g o n i e s
               erupt
flames of tearing
     down
          down
               down
ashes ashes
fire against the course of life
     shiny fears
     set amid the brightest night
not good for me
               no good
poison pumps within the veins
mortality takes
                    alluring luster
seducing
     flesh to ice
               our residence
away from day

- Brendan Tripp
01/04/1988

WITH EVEN DEATH DENIED

I can't
I am empty
there is no good
no use
struggles
run against a tide
which drives away
from hope
from caring
into void and lower realms

I fall blasted
made worse than death
isolated
alone, cut off
denied the comforts
common to the race

here lies my doom:
    shadows fall
    the dungeon walls
    are thick with slime
    the light now falters
    but not by death
    not in release

I pray for dying
I yearn for freedom
from this soul
from these chains
which lock me to this life
but there is never hope
no mercy is shown me
I am dying without death
rotting amid life

- Brendan Tripp
01/05/1988

THESE CYCLES OF RETURN

1
this rumbles in counterpoint
as illness trims the sail
and makes the going rough
within these channels

2
there are losings here
absences, though not explained
I am thick, no sense ensues
to allow for clearing sight

3
numbness enters to these vales
circumabulation's seed
a spinning that invades the mind
a cycle downward driven

4
impossibilities explode
as notions crumple small
there is some steel here gripping
there are no reasons made

5
what saves the night from fading
into comfort, cold and vague?
demand insists
against the exit flow

6
faceless voices hover round
the messengers of time
some shade of knowledge echoes here
within this presence felt

7
release is yet denied
the self and soul bear too much will
and lock to iron the spirit
now screaming to be free

- Brendan Tripp
01/06/1988

BROKEN DREAMS THAT NEVER FLY

descending
there is no hold
no locus to arrange a stay
the torrent sweeps
and drags us on
tumbling along the downhill wash
to all these endings

    drained,
    by panic frantic
    by anxiety frayed
    this the state
    in shallows limp
    this the backlash
    of hectic time

the script goes on
playing out the end of day
without attention
without much caring given
in wakes of drowning
in waking up to unseen light
strangely hovered low

    pain creeps
    into focus, sharp,
    made manifest
    in every voice
    or sight or fixture
    of the mind
    in tortured life

something here seeks to go
desires to leave
this chaos place insane
but every exit is well hid
or guarded by the brutal night
so locked to sorrow must it be
here shackled, doomed, unwell

- Brendan Tripp
01/07/1988

BECOMING SOMEHOW PULLED AWAY

the turning of the year
seems to suit
as new numbers bring
an altered set to day
it goes beyond
the moment held in reasoning
to new modes of employ
     and leaving comes
     too difficult to maintain
somehow this is alright
not burned down by cruel demand
in wasted seasons built to years
the alternatives do not await
but rush up screaming
     "this is the day"
without a purpose to define
but structured in a cluttered flow
so much the burden lately borne
against those modes of distance
     it comes to this
     unwilling now
which moment is the moment sensed
focus of this hanging dread
that wells from thoughts
of coming times
the brackets slip from presents
and scatter-shot these futures
that loiter ghostly
and so define out state
this can't be good
this ransoming to fear of times
not split from prophesy
or by some odds outlined
     warnings come all dressed in red
     not satisfied with simple feed
such devolves the time of flight
before the sky is rent
too much finds places poles apart
inscribing words in other days
to make the hour
bear for us such promised fruit

- Brendan Tripp
01/08/1988

THE CAUSE DISPLACED IN TIME

fewer become
advanced
swiftly these pass
as though
in flying be free
but there declines
the capacitance
within the shadows
of the clock
for forming all the well thought plans
it breaks down
it spins foulness
against the needy white
anguish, anguish,
there sobs from depths
a sorry soul
so wasted in the lonesome life
isolated, set apart,
as in dimensions
void but for itself
yet this too breaks
like mirrors' disfigurements
beset by bricks of rage
within the looming cloak of night
a violence flailing at the self
so hideously seen
days are stripped of use
for here is emptiness defined
in hollow grinding through the rites
so even absence bears its taint
like running sores
defiling temples of the sane
staining raiments falsely worn
in base pretense
lowly after might-have-beens
run far off on other lines
too far away to leave a scent
no, this is acting,
this is not a living life,
chaining on from night to day
in pointless roles which call for breath
where suicide would seem the key
to better scenes,
more noble plays,
less empty eyes and ashen gaze
denied the right to light

- Brendan Tripp
01/09/1988

SPLIT OFF FROM CENTER, MADE OF DAY

notes pull down
and break syntax
snowing paper, crying rain,
leading to the night of night
deleted from the absent count
seen on horizons
nearly here
unsettled but for briefest lines
of site and placing
of circling too long denied
a dust-like mote
born on cruel winds
that speaks to no-one
and of nobody leads
on through the winter
broken habit of the cold
left open, hanging,
creaking with the rust of age
despite reprisal
despite reviewing of the years
still set apart
awaiting spring
clouds still hover in the dark
boding of some close event
not yet in being
not quite within perception's net
but whispers waft
just beyond the ear on winds
which speak of settings
constructed to enable night
to fold within unfolding plots
of softer, warmer days than these
seen off beyond
sensed in some distant way
for here is passage
emptying the moment kept
of all its value,
content and intent,
made like a vacuum
to pull the future to the past
as though to grasp
the subtle straw of being

- Brendan Tripp
01/13/1988

ADJOINING COMMON GROUND

ice hangs
as breath is frozen
into frost
we circumambulate the park
calling visions
back to mind
making place transcend the time
and make this new
as once it was

here in shadows
are the graves
strange internments
scoured blank by years
whose passage clears the history
and wipes slate clean
rendering mute
but for the profile
but for the tilt
but for the promise of hard ground
that cradles these old bones
against the influence of steel
cement and smog
driving on beyond this place
sheltered niche
by centuries designed

newness folds
around the focus of return
infusing day
with manners of descent
here is protest
there are silent wishes made
within this going
amid these actions
scripted far away
interpretations
not held to any grade

- Brendan Tripp
01/14/1988

SHUTTLED THROUGH A STRANGER LAND

confused
dislocated
inhumanized beyond contempt
in strange horizons
places of unknowing wheres
I am stripped
of all equipment
disallowed the modes of ease

this going's mode
is strange of me
alien to common sense
here I am foreign
of other blood
stared at with downlooking eyes
accused in silence
so much apart

the view here might
be taken well
if from confusion
be relieved
but no
chaos is the reign
the king of places
of ill being

all plans decay here
assumptions go to rot
I know not places
I know not names
save heraldry fit for the sky
almost in tempting
somehow colluding
against this mind indeed

- Brendan Tripp
01/15/1988

THE JEALOUS DRIVE TO ART

1
but these are all the same
with no nuance thrown
to alter their demand
within the drive to art
it seeds in jealousy
and blooms frustration
it takes the form of squirming
against the perceived bounds
that seem delimitated
so to constrict the self
to tidier radii
not in justification
that cares for given time

2
at first the plot moves well
but illness enters
changes the assumed
    hours fly
    contact is not brought
    to modes of flesh
new scenes hatch
and brush runs brain to brain
almost in joining
    this too by clocks
    is run amok
    with distance riven

new days
come up
new faces
enter

and altered darkness
is the theme
here strange the link
    not made not ventured
    is the desired grasp
    which still awaits
location is awash in fear
stifled for the better show
crisp night brings walking
    we reach not
    but by these lines
    as hinting border

once more
return
again there
is loss

this will not work
the world becomes too close
uncomfortable, fingers fly
     the lure runs up
     eclipsing half the mass
     still blocking
there comes the threat again
beyond the harbors
place to which we flee
     it comes into length
     almost unwilling now
     it is time, then dark

3
communications
rides of place insane
daring cross the miles within
scope and span of easy light
what touches me of this?
the mind is shuffled,
is not made whole,
terror holds the simple themes
as years erase our toil
it comes again, again,
without the morbid echo
giving faith to course of day
in wasted, hollow ringing words
once good and of some future

- Brendan Tripp
01/18/1988

THE BROKEN OF THE OLD

and what has meaning
and what bears cause
there seem so few places
that give us entrance
that allow
a shedding of these chains
and a lifting of the veil
that holds us blindly
in some self-inflicted night
not free to open
not loose enough to spin
the visions that we know
deep within the mind

somehow
a crucial piece goes missing
a gap intrudes
that all our currents
can not jump
an emptiness invades the place
that would allow
the forming of new worlds

it all drops down to words
that swirl around
the nexus of intent
never reaching
the focus of our thought
never knowing
the crystal sharpness
that spreads across the night
and so infects
all other minds with light
so powerful
so clean

perhaps a death
should have become before
a sweeping tide to bring
reforming dark
     to take the scattered bits of I
     and cast them on the winds of time
     to settle in another place
     not burdened with a broken soul
perhaps a leaving
ran on some other line
that came and went
within some daylight
within some long ago
in better places
in sweeter fate

- Brendan Tripp
01/19/1988

ON SEEING BEEF TV

there opens up
some guilt in joy
that success might mean
real failure

I would wash these hands
clean of these days
as lucre runs red
in blood from slaughter floors
and stains my world
with poisoned deeds
these triumphant things
so tied up with death

     the snare is tightened
     and omens call
     from gory darkness
     so telling of these ways

I watch the blooming
of these bitter seeds
upon the dread and needed screen
there all these actions
charge with a thrill
which curdles into shame
of implications
disgusting to the soul

night opens into
brutal visions
there is no fleeing
from their sight

- Brendan Tripp
01/20/1988

SCATTERED, MADE TO SHINE

1
that will do
yes
I believe so
subtle is to simple
as these things
bring return

2
a call
intends another turn
brutal going
maybe sweet
there is aching there
there are the haunts of age

3
enough now
quite enough
capacitance is reached
long surpassed
the days switch over
to forced decline
wearily struggled with

4
strength ebbs
time seems a membrane
which resists
each moment's march
life is thick
movement hard
tomorrow seems
so far away

- Brendan Tripp
01/21/1988

WITHIN THE GOING

I find
long waits
in airports
nearly kill
the love of travel
this
combined with sickness
from the excesses of night
drive the spirit down

I await
the going to some deeper South
not held with expectation
for any good to come

I take myself
from city to city
forming wide and distant strokes
to my fourth-dimension form

I sometimes wonder
why these flows are lonely
why the lines can never meld
with others for some time
there are meetings
brief abuttings
where contact is so nearly made
but then again some force repels
and swings them far apart

I sometimes think
that maybe on one of these trips
some chance may turn things to the good
that lines of form
might meet and perhaps meld
to chart a better course
through time and space
made joyful

- Brendan Tripp
01/22/1988

THE STREETS OF JACKSON

how much alike
each of these cities seem
the streets of Jackson
could be the streets
of Appleton or Spokane
smaller places
where sidewalks come and go
where cars are sacred
and walking seems a crime
how strange this seems
to the major urban mind
that measures distance
in terms of blocks
and not in increments of time

in Manhattan or Chicago
these simple runs
would be no problem
no effort going point to point
separation figured
by lines on maps
or number of address
but in these lesser places
these are gulfs not crossable
abysses gaping
in hopeless voids
of industrial swamps
and freeway barricades
not fit for human feet

I grow so tired
when in these places
and yearn for canyons
of high cement and steel
the blissful chalices
of all real culture
those grey hard cities packed with life
whose pulse teems constant
so much unlike
the octane dribble of these towns
whose franchise being
is sham existence
and whose hollowness
stands devoid of mind

- Brendan Tripp
01/23/1988

MISSISSIPPI SUNDAY

there is dying here
fundamentalist rigor mortis
with empty Jesuses
in empty heads
that so believe the lie
that every truth
must be deformed
to fit the stupid cast of mind

fundamentalism is
the thrashing death throes
of an old and poisoned
view of God
struggling to enslave the soul
to withered, useless, hollow form
be it Christian, Moslem, Jew or Sikh
where conformation
to doctrines' words
eclipses all the spirit
and makes religion
into some Nazi parody
where everything plays like a skit
from Saturday Night Live In Hell
a shadow gulag
so filled with hate

so let us pray
for Armageddon
that we be delivered
from their old ways
that Earth be cleaned
and into newness brought

\- Brendan Tripp
01/24/1988

WITHIN THIS PLACE AWAY

1
better than I remember
an improvement over recall
or perhaps just that
this locale
is finer set
than any gone before

2
or that
the money being spent
buys better rent
with nicer things
to make the day
fly buy in luxury

3
occurrences occur
some make the ego
big and tall
twisting round
to pat it on its back
some make the ego
want to hide
twisting in,
contorting wholly
out of space

4
I like it here,
but where is here?
is this place
is this lodging
is this city, or domain?
I think I like the absence
the closeness leaving
the terror of real life behind

- Brendan Tripp
01/25/1988

DISCOMFORT TOWARDS THE DAWN

1
reach into
the black
of space
grasp nothing

plan into
the haze
of time
reach nothing

2
badness centers here
and still the curse
hangs beyond perception's glare
to poison life

a deep unwellness
hovers over every day
to cancel hope
and crush the soul

3
unknowing indicates the dark
pointing with its bony hand
and roughly scrapes the sores of fear
for the acid pus of dread

there is involvement with the day
conspiracy and treason
history peels off the hours
as enacting some intent

4
I did not know this
nor did I move those ways
the heart is blinded
empty and unsettled

hurtled is the eye
without their guidance
voided is the reason
that justifies such life

- Brendan Tripp
01/26/1988

WINTER ROAD WISCONSIN

unseasonable warmth
melts the snow
washes land with run-off
bares the sleeping earth
whose muted colors
have no names besides their own
straw and brush
withered grass
the palette seeding camouflage
cloaked as though to hide till spring

- Brendan Tripp
01/30/1988

FEBRUARY 1988

2/1/88	THE BUILDING OF THESE DAYS
2/2/88	SMASH DOWN THE WHOLE THING NOW
2/3/88	FROM THE ISOLATED GRAVE
2/4/88	THE WAY THEY SAY THE DAY
2/5/88	TO FLEE THIS AWFUL PLACE
2/6/88	PROVISION OF THIS YOKE
2/7/88	A FORM GIVEN TO DAY
2/8/88	NO FREEDOM, BRAKES, OR ROOM
2/9/88	BROKEN MOTION, GONE AWAY
2/10/88	SPIRAL DOWNWARD, AT ONE POINT
2/11/88	CENTERED SPLITTING SHAPE
2/12/88	FOCUS OF THE PLACE
2/13/88	RETURNING EMPTY
2/14/88	VISTA TORN IN LEAVING
2/15/88	NEWS IN OTHER ORDERS
2/16/88	OUR LAND UNFROSTED
2/17/88	PASTS UNRETURNED
2/18/88	JUST THIS FOR NOW
2/19/88	A PORTAL'S HAZE
2/29/88	LOST BETWEEN DAYS

THE BUILDING OF THESE DAYS

small going thus
tinge the light
night the sky
all awash
and touched by cold
that will not fly
denies the eye
as plans revert
to forms of warmth
and caring's lesser
modes observed
so tired asleep
these things rehearsed
while watching for the clock
there are too much
too many
more things fill up the day
cram hard the night
teem with fevered count
which scatter
multiply against the flow
insistent
demanding to be known

we would prepare
where preparation fails
set things aright
where only wrong can be

we seek some rest
amid the road of chaos
and reason in
the traps set for our being

- Brendan Tripp
02/01/1988

SMASH DOWN THE WHOLE THING NOW

there wants a crushing here
a tearing, shredding of these days
as hate evolves from these transgressions
spiteful barbs with acid points
that fly in blindness
bereft of thought
useless and insane

this poisons all within the world
it strips the nerves and lays them bare
all is conflict
all tinged with burning rage
goodness dies
and hope evaporates in dawns
of hideous unfiltered suns

these hands are stupid
made of flesh
they can not reach for throats
of these vague tormentors
to choke their sneering lives away
these demons of the mind
I yearn so much to slay

reality echoes these fires within
and slaps back hard against the self
it wants to kill
to slay and crush this soul
that dares to look beyond its bounds
and pray for leaving
invoke release

tear down this world
blast into dust these damning chains
rend from its whole
the universe to shreds
that I might be at peace
free from the madness of its sway
the human grind defining day

- Brendan Tripp
02/02/1988

FROM THE ISOLATED GRAVE

there is blockage
the trigger will not trip

from Her now alien
the voice, it is not heard

I am without
stepped beyond the bounds of earth
not in time
removed from this world

emotions lie withered, dead
yet I reach towards their putrescence

there is a spiral pulling down within
there is falling towards some darker state

this all seems ersatz
phony place to set my eyes
nothing's real
no concreteness hits my gaze

voids now reach and grasp these things
replacing absence for the known

doubt consumes the blood of spite
and feasts on guts eviscerated in this rage

I am unable to believe
there are no anchors for my trust
we move in shadows
mists of lies are all we're shown

grey blank engulfs life
solitude becomes the tomb

poisons come to kill the soul
spirit fades through murdered night

death would seem better
as hope deserts pointless existence
draining vitality
causing ashes to choke light

- Brendan Tripp
02/03/1988

THE WAY THEY SAY THE DAY

virtual
virtual
     seeming
          complete
numbing comes to minds
before
the hour empties lies
it all
          runs down
existential conjugation
with but one form to be
initialized
enslaved
     that is the
     the nexus
     the rub
          that is
now, here we have
is it not
colors flash from angle
light is turned to sand
     cycles run
     run return
returning to an altared state
altered in design
made vacant
as vacancies defined
               lit by neon
               flash on highway
                    distant night
          away
but run
     there pulls the bastard wheel
     which warps the phallic flow of time
returns
makes seeming walls against
our night
and whips sense from
intentive strikes
          here seen as able
          raising cane
for there are ways
of numbered thought
     two three
not virtual
not lied nor lent

- Brendan Tripp
02/04/1988

TO FLEE THIS AWFUL PLACE

sometimes
I wonder whether
being dead
is better than being alive

there are so many dead
so many
the majority
nearly all the race

the race
the stinking
putrid
hateful race

I want to purge
my humanity
wipe away my face
which is the face of man

I want to exit
from this god-damned world
leave all these stupid assholes
far behind

can death be worse
than the tortures found in life
a tempting question
since life aint working out for me

there is nothing
here for me
just cycles of damnation
reoccurrence of the curse

damn them all
damn their fucking world
I want to murder
to tear it down with fire

death is good
it is dark and sweet
it wraps its quiet
to muffle out the din

- Brendan Tripp
02/05/1988

PROVISION OF THIS YOKE

the hours
time
slips by
fading
I fade
weakness ensues
lateness encroaches
swirls of moments
form on the phone
lectured into these tomorrows
here now
undistant
these one time plans
are taken down
mind grows hazy
nearly vague
faces fade
names are mixed
uncertainty becomes the rule
as in these hours
all grows dark
dividing being
to absent ways

- Brendan Tripp
02/06/1988

A FORM GIVEN TO DAY

1
what is voided
in exertion
broken down
in these hours
drenched in sweat?

will rides up
against inertia
drives like whips
against a body
seeking rest

2
days have run
imagination
into foment
now put to test

are there coming
close connections
as spun by mind
for these hours?

too often when
these doors open
in unnamed terror
I'd step back

3
the spirit
runs broken
all echoes sadness
the unhealed wounds
of long ago

there is darkness
in this heart
there are curses
ringing in
these battered ears

- Brendan Tripp
02/07/1988

NO FREEDOM, BRAKES, OR ROOM

moments hidden
wash hits
from deep within
     strange
     druglike
labels become lost
all unknown
where from
does this proceed?
this whiteness
this sigh
     this falls
     against new day
yet denied
unfulfilled
ground between
the walls of time
pressing in
     closing
     tight
too many other things
demand
their din
wears down the brain
and snaps
the cord connecting
the link
     of mind
     and world
they seek some center
some violent point
I stand
target
focus of the lethal blows
screaming
from the strain within
shrinking
     away from earth
     out from the world
all goes black
everything dies
motion stills
stiffens
and grows cold

- Brendan Tripp
02/08/1988

BROKEN MOTION, GONE AWAY

things come strained
mind rushes to decay
and so
as such
not really very much
falls down to die
in suicide
broken
crushed and crumbled
strewn amok
scattered
to the nether realms
herewith beside
a reason
to leaving
in different context
stranger ways
I go
exeunt
habituate the absent
got with getting out
a falling down
a dropping path
fading
folding
like to die
the final act
the termination here
brought into sharper
focus
brighter light
screaming
blinding
burning bright
loosed without heart
so beyond care
all undefined
so unaware

- Brendan Tripp
02/09/1988

SPIRAL DOWNWARD, AT ONE POINT

nothing changes
nothing
    but time strips off
    the veil of newness
    and makes things old
    to wither and die
almost identical
here I make a close return
four years on
and echo words from that before
strangely hollow in this night

    everything goes
    into changing
    yet nothing changes
    just decays

- Brendan Tripp
02/10/1988

CENTERED SPLITTING SHAPE

expansion
must come
amid denial
and the tardy place

enlargement
grows within
altered dates
to form rebuttal
to answer to despite
and lash to being
the later form...

- Brendan Tripp
02/11/1988

FOCUS OF THE PLACE

1
rise up before light
experience the cycles
of the sun

lateness brings twinkles
city lost
in distance

other lights accentuate
flying pierces
these environs

    2
    plans drop down
    no good
    acts grow useless
    empty
    dictates are held
    as king

3
fortune
is not here
befuddled
is the mind
spaces grow
wide grow small
shifting context
cripples
makes unsure
makes unaligned
    makes day come early
    and night die late
in retrograde
devolutions and decay

- Brendan Tripp
02/12/1988

RETURNING EMPTY

drastic void
drastic
simple absence
makes the grade
and death
sways up on winds
not calm
not cooling
this rides ending
and fortifies
the bare decay

- Brendan Tripp
02/13/1988

VISTA TORN IN LEAVING

above rides
high
near soulless
ancient peels the ground
beating ages with the wing
of absent rivers carved
all grey
ashen
brown to dust
too old
run from presents backwards
screaming towards the past
such is return
ebbing from one action
into channels of the new
we are transient
unheld by moments
passing, ephemeral
torn forward forever
piercing time

here more going
washed of color
lateness folds against our line
and anticipates the ache
to come by hours
distance and strange will
madness is allowed
all fire and ruddy
bursting out in cruel confine
not given defense
not able to support
it flows to power
and is disrupted
so corrupt

- Brendan Tripp
02/14/1988

NEWS IN OTHER ORDERS

1
desire fires blindly
into black
with no mode
of target acquisition
no way to guide
the madly spinning need

2
abrupt
inert
inconsequent
beside
without
ephemeral
afar
beyond
transitional

3
names are not assigned
ignorance pleads abject
the entrance is unfound
destruction's maw gapes open

darkness calls to seed
enveloping the world
senses fade to absence
isolation and dull grey

4
habitation
extracts
makes
evident
manners
of being
modes
of
new pain
there are
here
the forms
unknown
unseen
unbearing

\- Brendan Tripp
02/15/1988

OUR LAND UNFROSTED

these are
we are
not those
they are of the fields and forest
they know seasons and their pulse
we are
solid
we are frozen steel
we have mighty concrete muscles
that tear away the trees and grass
and make things grey
purified and still
they do not wake
they do not see
the brutal rise of dawn
splash red and orange on thrusting spires
as sky-born lamps cede to their master's day
on silent streets
on sidewalks wet from night
no, they do not know,
these other ones,
they live with life
and breathe the puling of its ways
their mornings come with waking things
that scream the beatitudes of earth
before they start the killing dance
of the feeding and the fed
we are
so far
so driven from those ways
as morning brings the surging race
in sweats of madness
headlong in an alloy dream
so tightly focused to be gone
into the realms of sun-seared night
we are
the real
not like
the simpering course of man
locked crying in the garden's ash

- Brendan Tripp
02/16/1988

PASTS UNRETURNED

photos of
the faraway
drawing at parts
left behind
traces etched
into the fabric
of the weave
of wider worlds
deeper than
the lines of time

there are touches
felt from these
that invade
the heart or mind
or in between
somehow beyond
felt within
bits that cling
of places entered
long ago

how would we reach
back to these visions
and take them up
experiencing
the currents of
these crossings
denied by misty
veils of age
these points defining
space and time

- Brendan Tripp
02/17/1988

JUST THIS FOR NOW

here we are
staring at an empty screen
again;
and again
there is nothing,
nada,
el blanko

you wonder where
the mind goes
when you dip in the well
and come up with a bucket of dust...
it's like swishing around in thin air
where there ought to be
some thick broth filled with succulent chunks
of wit, wisdom, agony or despair

but no,
sometimes there is only void,
the kind of empty left in a room
when the residents
have up and left
and the new folks haven't
followed the painters through

hell,
it's a wonder that
anything gets done
when that breeze runs through
from ear to ear;
I just want to sit
and watch the traffic flow
and forget the "musts"
as the world goes by

- Brendan Tripp
02/18/1988

A PORTAL'S HAZE

the spectre
of departure
arises
the vision
of change
becomes

    there are mountains beyond
    crisp with wind by sky wiped clean
    awaiting going
    anticipating arrival

here comes the silence
the onset of the absent word
I feel its approach
like the queasy edge of on-rushing storms
a lip folded over from the dark
which holds as secret many days

    there plummeting go I
    as rattling these hours cease
    their separation
    from immediacy

the season
of translation
uncovers
the moment
of turning
arrives

- Brendan Tripp
02/19/1988

LOST BETWEEN DAYS

these are places
defining distance
the hollow shells
of far aways
yet these too fall
under the sway of self
and lie corrupted
below the open moon

the prayer of breaking
seems absurd
against those phantom ego chains
the shell is massive
hideous and strong
yet through its fractures
we glimpse that crystal light
and so struggle on

towards this leaving
we have gone
made voyages to nights beyond
the balance of the day
we are anticipation
a quiver and a hope
that by this shadow lighting
real change may plant a seed

it almost comes to ending
almost reaches cycles through
the gates of time
sketched into fullness by the miles
taken out to wider ways
that may yet blossom
to bear the fruit
of life repurified

- Brendan Tripp
02/29/1988

MARCH 1988

3/7/88 THE FIRST WAY BACK TO NEWNESS
3/8/88 THOSE COME TO CHANGING
3/9/88 FOR DAYS STREWN OFF
3/10/88 THE OFFICE OF REJECT
3/11/88 TO BLINDED MOVE UNGUIDED
3/13/88 DISTRACTING CYCLES SPRUNG
3/14/88 HARD SET BY TIME
3/15/88 ALL THE SIDES TO PLACE, TO TIME
3/16/88 ALONE BEFORE THIS WIND
3/17/88 ERUPTED IN THIS PLACE
3/18/88 BECOMING LEGEND BY AND BY
3/19/88 DESCENT THROUGH NIGHTS TO DAY
3/21/88 PROBLEMS BORN TO SIGHT
3/23/88 BARELY TOUCHING ON THE TIME
3/24/88 CURSED TO EXILE FROM ALL LOVE
3/25/88 THAT NAME, THAT NUMBER FACED
3/26/88 IN SNAPSHOTS OF THE GOING
3/27/88 GONE THROUGH THESE TO RETURN
3/28/88 BLEED CHANNELS OF THE MIND
3/29/88 CALENDARS THROUGH FOLLY SET
3/30/88 THE NAGGING CUBE OF B

THE FIRST WAY BACK TO NEWNESS

this settles not
all things are blown to farthest reach
and borders wrap the universe
so undefined

I have no name
all that has happened is now of dust
ground to ashes of the fire
there is no course
but of these "not" things guided
to hazy lands

I seem alone
yet feel the tugs of new connection
like lines that limit aimless drift
so forms the North
in crystal matrix
which grows the tribe to seed the East

my ears now search
and rake the silence
praying for whispers to somehow form
the words of knowing
the mantle of the conscious way
so far apart

here come the days
that shall standardize renewing
evolving faces, bodies, selves,
out of this fog

- Brendan Tripp
03/07/1988

THOSE COME TO CHANGING

dance upon this pyre
by moonlight
dance
sing within these walls
by starlight
sing

die from all your past
in union
die
call to all your tribe
in honor
call

know the open door
of changing
know
act the final rite
of passage
act

turn in subtle coils
to newness
turn
blast through crystal form
to greatness
blast

- Brendan Tripp
03/08/1988

FOR DAYS STREWN OFF

there comes a calling
from mists of doubt
a calling comes

it is the tribe

return has fractured oh so much
made madness seek its own relapse
here in the mind
residing loosely
hung slightly by those cords now cut
and not reformed
by silver bands

I search that face
I search this name

going makes its siren call
so soon again
so soon
I search within to find the clue
to chart the schedule of those days
but am yet lost
am yet denied the clarity
that seem to shine beyond my reach

and there within
gleams crystal

new being hovers
close within, familiar, strange
it captures reign
and opens up new doors of self
far gone from day
as so beyond that not by mind itself
be seen
or sensed or known
only in echoes of vast machines
it comes to light
the clanging of the arcane works
now chugging off behind the soul

somewhere within the tribe now calls
in forming of the shining self

- Brendan Tripp
03/09/1988

THE OFFICE OF REJECT

before this storm breaks
before the echoes of confusion ring
let there come voice
let there be the thunder of decree
shaking down these walls so vain

options scatter in this wake
making reason act the slave
there is no ticket, no final price
that hampers this the arcane run
now loosed from temples long on high
in avalanche it redefines

and I reject, disavow
your form and purpose
your ways and means
these were my masters long before
the chaining weights that would not free
me in your day
but I have grown the wings of darkness
and have wrapped myself in the cloak of death
to be my comfort
and my escape

so now apart I stand
your maddened dictates do not faze
the steady eye that stares
into your world from far beyond
you are the looking glass insane
a sweaty nightmare
of some long gone sleep
long rubbed from out these eyes

go back to blankness
back to the void
you are the phantasms of failure
I have no dealings with your world
but for these shadow symbols here
that soon shall pass
that soon shall fade
and settle in the mists of dream

- Brendan Tripp
03/10/1988

TO BLINDED MOVE UNGUIDED

from there we move on
taking abrupt the bitter pill,
seed to prayer,
and in confession make new maps
and pen the world afresh

I seek the blade
to sever all this clinging life
which hangs putrescent
wrapping with decayed embrace;
there must be clearness,
these must be clean,
lopped smoothly from the growing limb

how does one speak
this banishing?
how do the words create
that separation
and forge such absence as would free
the soul from grasping shell?

it knows that well
by symbols deep within,
yet utters silence to the plea,
hooded, stark,
as though expectant of some sign
to open tomes
and light the way to probing minds

thus steel the centers
and so invoke
the lineage of all our tribe
to shed this darkness
and pierce the veil of future life

- Brendan Tripp
03/11/1988

DISTRACTING CYCLES SPRUNG

1
against these images
spun out in face of night
old ways resume
full to flesh
strange in their return

2
this is not named
not handles by the mind
the four-fold grid evaporates
into some other plane
and leaves us solo in the dark

3
our dimension
becomes no good
it decays to solids
and is no more awing,
embattled by the real
it slaps to the concrete
and roars an echo
across our time

4
some switch gets thrown
inside the mind
that operates the gates of space
between the worlds
sometimes it closes
hard clanging with despite
and locks us in
orphans to our vision

- Brendan Tripp
03/13/1988

HARD SET BY TIME

it comes down
to written words
drops again
to pages white
this is a madness
an untamed creeping meme
which runs its fibers
through the brain
and lights up memories and rhyme
now long to dust
ground down to brittle age
locked in irons
and plastic case
for duty and the deed

    (can not be sent
     in hours' time,
     can not allow
     the spread to be)

in this am lost
I am
the structured point
of other being
yet lack dimension here
and so to scream
so to panic
against the chains alone we see
that fetter to the binding world
now felt constricting
blinding and malicious
bent upon our own demise
once thought declared
once sure to be

- Brendan Tripp
03/14/1988

ALL THE SIDES TO PLACE, TO TIME

1
it is decay where nothing matters
a tidal pool of no escape
where stillness silences all action
and hope evaporates to dread
2
there seems floating from
that place
there appears separation
as though a ghost
hovering did watch
informing on
the scene enacted
3
how might one expect this coming
given history and fate
4
I don't know
I am as much the audience
as actor
the stage holds me without a script
5
who has being,
who cradles essence
to ownership?
6
the segments are delineated
yet still the vision blurs
not willing to pierce time
or open to the greater seeing
it is this way
in every aeon
it always is the same
7
mirrors present
the swell of years,
nearly bursting
in a rain of broken glass
8
delay those forms of reasoning
accepting the decision
9
whirlwind spins
cycle spiral though;
here is now, triumphant

- Brendan Tripp
03/15/1988

ALONE BEFORE THIS WIND

finding what's important
what has meaning
what is real
delving into sides of life
that are uncharted
strange and without name
so comes the dawning
of new age
here arrives the call
hard breaking like the dawn

the words of others
so confuse
they turn about
like spinning games
of vertigo
and splay the center
into smears now undefined
somehow unreal
and lost upon the shifting tides
of merciless retreat

but other words come unexpected
and bring strange joy
piercing veils of isolation
shocking smiles
from steady states of grey
these are the servants of the muse
and must so be attended
they speak from unknown pasts
and seem the harbingers
of some future promise made

yet all descending falls
each instance rises in its time
to wither, die, and fade
from memory, reality
becoming myth or lie
told in the twilight
of this perceptive life
spent in illusion's grasp
a solitary sparkle
held to the face of dark

- Brendan Tripp
03/16/1988

ERUPTED IN THIS PLACE

headlong into destruction
break down now
it's the death party
it's the death trip
it is history and location
imagination and insane
flowering in madness
seeded by the dissonance
of being and its cage
so much perceived at present
to breakdown comes
evolving fractures to the self
schisms deep within the mind
that seep the lava
burning, glowing deep with rage
with hatred steeped in darkest fire
the flowing abhorrence
of all the entries of this life
pointillisticly despised

a vile revulsion sweeps this face
into the trash heap of decay
rejecting all it means
discarding all its world
from unknown centers comes a glee
that pulses with destruction
and spins the whirlwind in its dance
like Shiva crushing all
breaking down the old for new
this wantonness seeks to erase
the lingered self
the lagging being
those gross reminders of old life
now given up
tossed into pyres to die
disowned and blasted
exiled shade disgraced
broke down to ashes
and purified by fire

- Brendan Tripp
03/17/1988

BECOMING LEGEND BY AND BY

this assumes destiny
it shuttles pages beyond
their normal scope and realm
asking questions of definition
brushed aside by hazards of the mind
until the closing comes
and insurrections feed their fires
the stuff of being
harbored in the secret times
against the tide of deep regret
now surging at the bastions
and threatening new modes of depth
washed impossibly below
to redefine the course of place
to that occulted
made to lurk beneath the mass
of ancient oceans not allowed
the visits of the light
and form the whispers of new dark
set out upon the earth
to echo in the starry night
a lore unfounded
a mystery that won't avail
to probes based on the reasoned measure
pressed hard upon the yielding flesh
of racial memory
here live the purposes of time
the grids that form the base
of every pattern
every vector given man
to charge and scatter
to dream and fear and hope and care
all built on nothing
but the wind
or shifts within the swirling murk
not yielding answers
nor optioning the asking word

- Brendan Tripp
03/18/1988

DESCENT THROUGH NIGHTS TO DAY

split the dark
schism night
force dawn from hours
undenied
draining blackness
into blue

and alone
once more
so much against intent
as though the curse
again would prove
its own existence
denying us the rights of man

never comes
that fateful day
awaited through these years
that breaks the spell
unlocks the door of solitude
and opens up new modes of self
that are entombed
here in this lonely place

- Brendan Tripp
03/19/1988

PROBLEMS BORN TO SIGHT

from here
this darkness spreads

    is this the line
    by time defined?

clattering
options shift in place
spreading branches
impossible to encompass

    are there trends here,
    can pattern be discovered?

days empty out of promise
and blow off dry as husks

    will winning come
    before decay?

shattered form denies
the drive of pressing will
with mutinous stasis
tolling into ruts of sloth

    is hope unfounded,
    drained of reason and insane?

the face turns grimly
and sets to steel the unsure aim

    are visions doled
    to only fools?

lightning splinters,
crystal forms as by decree;
captured ethers rise
to be the norm

    will this make futures
    shine stronger than the violent sun?

- Brendan Tripp
03/21/1988

BARELY TOUCHING ON THE TIME

there is nothing there
but the background hum
of words moving across time
to make this afternoon unique
     to wrest from it
     some gem-like fortune
     of incisive sight
there are cycles
and counter cycles
running here
vectors drag direction
into futures undefined
     all at the moment
     all at once and overlaid
     the helm is blurred
good may from those hours come
but just beginning now
a sentence without jail
self manacled to duty
     the screen within the head
     flashes, channels change
     video churns to chaos
dreams form of lucre
gushing cash against all odds
what are the numbers
make them mine
not awake without the dream
     shocking, modes change
     brutality shifts gears
     opens eyes to meanness
will there be a going
a freeing knowledge given
that will uncloud the day
and make the night divine?
     we option distance
     and make our absences real
     in vapor and decay

- Brendan Tripp
03/23/1988

CURSED TO EXILE FROM ALL LOVE

flirting with depression
for lack of other options
while lurching on the brink
of that all too known abyss

the brutal numbers rise
always viler with increase
they thrust into the brain
and tear apart the spirit

the heart is agonized
as the soul sinks lower down
the world is veiled in dark
and bears a death-like pallor

the questions come to whys
and cycle back to asking
no answers do they bring
just spirals of new anguish

the days and nights count down
their totals of rejection
they build beyond belief
these vast structures of despair

against the yearn to die
wells a living tide of rage
that feeds the soul with hate
for that tainted spiteful race

this poisons every sight
and disinters suspicion
for every simply act
and every word mistaken

I wish to step away
to leave this loveless focus
but facts act as my chain
my prison of denial

all lies are spoke of love
of goodness and emotion
this is a place of Hell
a dungeon and a torment

- Brendan Tripp
03/24/1988

THAT NAME, THAT NUMBER FACED

whoa, shocking
from out of all these names
returning here
here comes one face
     an absent face
     so long denied
for which I scarcely have a name
the tracks so burned
that memory is scarred
from trying to forget
but there it is
smiling, not in trail
of any of its kind
     a treasure, this
     a keepsake and remembrance
still do I feel
all flesh has not turned
hardened by the pain
and I respond
almost hoping to erase
long months of absence
begging to reach out
     across the chasm
     between her path and mine
but here I know
the folly of such hope
I see the fading edges of that form
as drifting off it waves to me
not seeking contact
or some reprieve
     this is saluting
     a bouquet at the grave
yet here I stand
still stunned with this delight
unsure of whether
this laughter should be cries

- Brendan Tripp
03/25/1988

IN SNAPSHOTS OF THE GOING

1
there are no destinations
here
no vectors pointing
to completion
only movement
only going
absenting one place and time
in exchange for yet another

2
so far away
power lines lead
from towers clustered
cluttering sight
like oil found and extracted
like forests wrought of steel
off in pointless distance
unfamiliarly strange

3
light plays angles
of early morning
almost unremembered
shadows set this way
promising illumination
the death of clouds and rain

4
here comes cloaking
enveloping the day
as stripes fly by
pulsing forward against the clock
beating schedules fragmented
ripped within the lowered sky

5
there sings somehow
of spirit leaving
floating detached from form
wafting strongly to the ends
of journeys lightly made
easy in the pleasant breeze
unhindered by old life

- Brendan Tripp
03/26/1988

GONE THROUGH THESE TO RETURN

1
all things go wrong
plans dissipate
totals rack beyond our ken
unknowing in some dark beneath
the veil of time
the cloak of night
a horror hid for new surprise

2
be stupid going
allow the weight of sleep
to cook you in these seats
so unprepared
for cramming ride
wrapped in layers for the wind
which will not stir within

3
desolation, empty, void
the streets run hard to streetlights' gleam
denied the wash of cars
among these others
awaiting stand
in strange surround defined by night
and by its creatures
made unsafe to stay
at last
find exit in fulfilled need
and flee to realms of light

4
settle down to that demand
that whips the days to rank
and paints them purple
regal in their self-despite
a turned insult, a mirror sneer
that coils within again
and counts the numbers
enumerates the depth and breadth
and locks our time away

- Brendan Tripp
03/27/1988

BLEED CHANNELS OF THE MIND

there stands the absence
switched over by the chronicle
of departed things coming back
drifting soundly though the distance of the night
contained in darkness
all discomforts of wrong time
confusing thought in shallow grasp
that knows nothing of the real

this comes up acid
like vomit on the walls of no control
etching maladies in the record of the place
scenting years with trails of pain
which reels in remembering
somehow vague, hazy, blurred
a sea of scenes through which to swim
to find the truth of history

stuttering events decay
each to their individualistic frame
held outside the flow of time
as though a window to the world
not linked by bricks into a whole
these float in limbo
and can not build a life
or forge a course of being

this state is poison
damaged and unwell
all growth is pruned to death
all vitalness is drained away
we are abstraction
a theory and not real
as though our dreamer
had lost the reins of sleep

still there occurs the breaking
where madness rips the steel of tawdry day
like thunder tearing clear blue skies
and shocks the open gaping eyes
of robot clowns to vision
cry for this seeing
weep oceans for this violation
of reality and stares

- Brendan Tripp
03/28/1988

CALENDARS THROUGH FOLLY SET

there settles into being
schemes
filling days with dreams of pain
well beyond the now
scraping at the aching sores
of future torment set to be
we enter
the corridors of time unseen
with heedless daring
and stupid glee
traipsing foolish
set to naught
so unawares of what might lie
within the underbrush of life
in lurking dark
close shadowing our steps
as waiting signals when to pounce
when weakness opens up the door
and we falter
prey to slipping stone
and treacherous footing of the path
alas
these are snares we set ourselves
booby traps we know too well
     their acute angles
     foreshadow our demise
     their acid seething
     sounds echoes of our end
there is no learning
no chance for clear reform
no hope
for real redemption in this life
     so held to vile decay
     and weakness of the spirit
so to these cycles
we return
and make the circuit once again
pointing at these years in chain
as existential evidence
proving that indeed we be
as doubt might still
be harbored at our pain
paraded through these killing days

- Brendan Tripp
03/29/1988

THE NAGGING CUBE OF B

now here goes
the saying
detaching
from the place
of the ride
in those new
afternoons
like return
long ago
not desired
expected
we go off
on the run
needing not
the mission
yet there are
other things
forcing us
into modes
obeying
orders that
grind our teeth
split the skull
but without
an escape
no options
no plan "B"
only "A"
or else "Z"
just conform
or destroy
just submit
or release
all the wrath
rage and hate
dammed up from
many years
holding to
these dictates
forcing down
our own will
to yet keep
terminal
chaos out
of the world
around us

- Brendan Tripp
03/30/1988

APRIL 1988

4/4/88	CRASHING INTO EMPTY LIFE
4/5/88	LOST BETWEEN THESE STATES
4/6/88	OUT OF PRESENTS SPUN
4/7/88	IN THE PAPER'S WAKE
4/8/88	THE CENTER HERE UPSET
4/9/88	PIECES HEWN OF DAY
4/10/88	THE FIRST FEW SCANS OF CHAOS
4/11/88	ONE ACT TO MAKE THEM DIE
4/12/88	THE POISONED, HOLLOW, PLACE OF LIFE
4/13/88	CODES DERIVED FROM INTERSECTS
4/14/88	IN CRUSHED TOMORROWS
4/15/88	WHAT'S TRUE SEEMS NEVER GOOD
4/18/88	TO RUE THE SUMMER DREAM
4/19/88	SEEING JOY AND NERVES ENTWINED
4/20/88	CRUSHED AGAIN, IN DISBELIEF
4/21/88	LOST IN RUSHING TIME
4/25/88	IN CHAPELS OF THE FLAME
4/26/88	YET MISSING YOUR EMBRACE
4/27/88	BROUGHT FORTH AGAINST THE NIGHT
4/28/88	RUN DOWN THROUGH EMPTY YEARS
4/29/88	THE FOOL AWAKES AGAIN

CRASHING INTO EMPTY LIFE

there comes nothing by this way,
the whirlwind dies
leaving ashes, aching in its wake;
each day makes sickness
more intense,
poisoning the total world

there are no names,
all is shed with aging;
we hold back violence,
just contained,
as madness might erupt and break
the fragile structure of this life

counts decry a number's curse
and flay again the bloody soul
which hides from hateful blasts
of self-born spite and loathing
so seeking absence,
so desperately pursuing death

the matrix of the earth is broken,
the fragments of our time decay;
this is our sentence,
this is the foul enchantment
which makes us agonized
without hope of escape

there must be leaving,
a sloughing off of this poor life,
each day drains bloodless
in useless fight against the dark;
somewhere in shadows
perhaps will hide our light

can any of these flights
be said to frame that newness?
we see no guarantee
to seed the hope to muddle on
through days of torment
and nights of broken dreams

- Brendan Tripp
04/04/1988

LOST BETWEEN THESE STATES

there it goes
again
the vacillation
between old
and new
swinging from extremes
     of desperate life
          where darkness harbors
          all despair
     to hazy visions
          of evolution,
          growth and light
how I want
to see
a vector forward
a current
a trend
away from this hell

some focus
needs come
some name or language
to direct
these days
into crystal dawns
     in this I stumble
          unknowing manners
          of the clear
     my acts seem useless
          and cycle downwards
          to the murk
still this wall
divides
me from the brightness
while knowledge
stains me
different from the dark

- Brendan Tripp
04/05/1988

OUT OF PRESENTS SPUN

no words
time flies
mind is blankness
frantic, dead
all churns to futures
now is denied
we see things
through glass
in mirrors
not quite present
hardly real
somehow distant
at removes
so far
from here
divorced
from focus
of this time
of this where
that is the world
the universe
that spins
that whirls
all around
never crystal
yet ungrasped
a haze, a blur
a whipping scene
like carousel outsides
whipping by
at a thousand R.P.M.
some blending madness
confusing mind

- Brendan Tripp
04/06/1988

IN THE PAPER'S WAKE

where creeps
the fundamental curse
across the bleeding globe
     from town to town
     the minds shut down
as madness' seeds
drift upon the air
churning violence
into a froth of gore
     their little brains
     ignoring pain

blindness locks
a grid of ignorance
upon the masses' sight
     stupid lying
     faithful dying
as every doctrine
arms its fools
with steel forged in hate
and passions of deceit
     armies attend
     the coming end

time twists
into a tourniquet
to staunch the flow of thought
     these empty eyes
     believe the lies
as priests and mullahs
excite the frenzy
and rabbis ferment
the plots of coming doom
     preaching gory
     same old stories

darkness clouds
the burning firmament
that leaders claim as sky
     hollow words blast
     changing the past
as poison grips the soul
of fevered states
corrupting all men
and murdering the world
     a dying place
     a useless race

- Brendan Tripp
04/07/1988

THE CENTER HERE UPSET

useless acts
run the day down
as illness' waves
wash over this form
unwell
unwell
not fit for moving
hours on
into longer afternoons
and evenings of
uncounted plans

where is purpose
in the world?
where does untainted
guidance hide?
there seems no pattern,
no reason in the flow
and all is empty,
drained of goal,
just random thrashings
of fleeting forms,
the mindless moves
of the not quite dead

and now night wraps
uncaring arms
around its children
and offers doubt brought from afar
to nauseate them
through her passage
fearful
weeping
this darkness stabs the soul
and bleeds it empty
hollow as the wind

\- Brendan Tripp
04/08/1988

PIECES HEWN OF DAY

1
images are fixed in stealth
steering darkness into sleaze
the chained mind wanders
into fever's fits
spilling secrets
in the places we deny

2
rules align
in new manners form
fear lifts as mists
as details come to view
a startling scene
at first in doubt

3
two agendas ride here
one insists of things to do
the other shadows boredom
as though the list
were not enough
and hours longer than the day

4
anticipating season
reach beyond these walls
but there is ice yet hung in air
and cutting edge yet in the wind
so scurry back to warmth
and still in safety hide

5
the other splits a spectrum
into phases, names,
each on a different wavelength hoped
as though in separate worlds
if only coming time would split
to calendars for each

- Brendan Tripp
04/09/1988

THE FIRST FEW SCANS OF CHAOS

then amazed
not often amazed
any more
pictures
pretty pictures
brightly colored
abstract forms
with frames showing
blocks that then
become the next
pretty picture
no less complex
than the last
with new colors
convoluting
into strange swirls
and new frames
showing segments
that are now
the following
pretty picture
each step deeper
each step somehow
finer, smaller,
yet every step
is the same
in detail
and format
spraying chaos
ever inward
towards some nothing
dragging sense
down tunnels filled
with light and color
ever falling
deeper in
to pretty pictures
brightly colored
abstract forms
equations patterned
for the mind

\- Brendan Tripp
04/10/1988

ONE ACT TO MAKE THEM DIE

death rings up
expressing self as rage
and makes the juxtaposition
of self and site
intolerable
so that one must go
or parts of both
be shredded off
into some nonexistence
death of this place
death of this self
the screaming death of stupid fools
idiots who press on me
make me foam a sea of blood
and stare as though
they do not know
their central, damning, killing guilt

why hasn't death
freed me from this?
how can these universes
so unlike
still jostle in the same space,
duplicating coordinates
competing till the death?

these are the times
when blades seek me
when hate of others
turns into suicidal frenzy
when all the world
just feeds the loathing
burning blacker than hell's rage
and there is no clear place to strike
no lethal spot to make it die
and in frustration
the hate curls in
to slay the self that sees their world
to break the weakest link
obliterating
the fleshy feeling I
that is so tortured by this rage
sinking to darkness
warm and cloaking
calm and absent
so simple and so far away

- Brendan Tripp
04/11/1988

THE POISONED, HOLLOW, PLACE OF LIFE

darkness
where the rage ebbs
and soundtracks play
long buried songs
other's words
of dear import
here are the shallows
the stormset lees
of crushing brought to bear
the spent exhaustion
much like release
but by poison rinsed
anointed vile
in here festers
tidal pools
that breed strange vermin
subtle beasts that lurk inside
and shift the focus
from good to bad
that seem to filter
our minds and eyes
to only see the hues of hate
and make days ragged
and out of synch
to grind discordance
upon the mind
smothering
the growth towards light
casting shadows
shivering in grey and blue
a sickly world
a wan and weakened place
now drained of anger
empty of all sure design
but for resentment
and a vengeance that
abides its time

- Brendan Tripp
04/12/1988

CODES DERIVED FROM INTERSECTS

1
death walks so near
2
neo-Luddites
interrupt the flow
and break against
refreshment
3
suspension places
gaps amid involvement
4
we question days
not holding for a reason
yet crave some order
some purpose and some light
5
new names are given her
6
confusion agitates the mind
which sinks in swirling fog
and paddles aimless
unsure and without guide
7
the veil is lifted
as season manifests its change
8
into darkness
not my own
opacity
of borrowed kinds
9
within desire is need
10
brutality handles
the scheduled course
of futures chained
into the distant haze
11
this separation
evolves towards ending
12
the portal looms before
as though a riddle and a test
daring its passage
and tempting in its scents

- Brendan Tripp
04/13/1988

IN CRUSHED TOMORROWS

ready for absence
made of days denied
inception becomes
flowed through these hours
inverted within
their scans of being

it has arrival
accomplishes scenes
of apparition
and engulfs the air
with palpable night
to ends of leaving

knowledge seeps empty
the crucible spills
the stuff of plans out
soiling the planet
with pollutant streams
of aimless action

there is no reaching
all touching is banned
curtains of distance
divide up this space
creating new laws
unwritten, unfair

apart this hastens
draws up lines of strife
to tear asunder
need and hope and dreams
all becomes schism
broke before the deed

so falls the kingdom
fading in the mist
another empire
crumbled into dust
receding visions
built of clouds and tears

- Brendan Tripp
04/14/1988

WHAT'S TRUE SEEMS NEVER GOOD

anticipation
opens wide
from shrouds
all things uncover
into change
made new and clear
in foolish hope
not crystal
more of pictures made
that shift the hours
of our time
and realign
the course of day
this seeds without
and is not of
the inner churn
set madly distant
and indistinct
we fear to enter
to touch that ghostly way
that seems to beckon
us in these weeks
and promise
a great unfolding
of joy unknown for long
in words so suspect
from shadows of the mind
not trusting goodness
not willing
to suspend our disbelief
and float on maybes
into the teeth
of cold displeasure
seen malicious
in the world
waiting, lurking
once again

- Brendan Tripp
04/15/1988

TO RUE THE SUMMER DREAM

there shadows the summers
of the mind
summers not known
by self
but summers made of dreams
and jealous longings
for those careless joys
so apart from this dark life

age creeps up
and makes a joke of "this year" thoughts
now that good times' time is passed
and new gulfs widen
between realities
and those sweet fantasies of heat
no longer just denied by love
but also now by life

summer wraps cruel isolation
around the inner self
whose mind is torn between the pulls
of wariness and want
each cycle forming
new limits to our worth
each question asking
when cursed became this life

still hope infects
the hidden corners of the soul
where poison has not reached
a sorry hope of stupid dreams
of summers filled with love and laughs
not frozen in the ice
of long rejection
the chilling bane of life

- Brendan Tripp
04/18/1988

SEEING JOY AND NERVES ENTWINED

eyes touch
what hands have not
straining, yearning to deploy
against such suppleness
seeking for the angle
to open up to sight

I am lost
plummeting beyond the edge
desire has tipped
the balance kept
between cold reason
and this throbbing heat

a single slice of time
so filled is this
with old a new
places near and places far
frustration huddles in the whirl
not knowing where to turn

each darkness brings new lines
fresh scenes unacted
to try to force the day
into the patterns of our need
so long in exile
in dungeons of despite

here is the body
the flesh of dreams returned
to haunt the waking
and lock with unnamed scent
away the mind
into patterns of all age

these prayers come layered
in confusion spilled
all out at once
an insane tumult formed of want
mad for the sating
they scream for the completing ease

- Brendan Tripp
04/19/1988

CRUSHED AGAIN, IN DISBELIEF

so it goes
like that again
no one believes
how this can be
not even me

which night comes
not lonely,
when is solitary
not the dawn?

what causes
this flight from me
what poison causes
equations to deflate
where time and place
and persons seem right
and yet the script
falls through the fingers
of our shock
reverting once again
to patterns of rejection
of denial and belittlement
turning something pleasant
into something cruel and sick
an endless cycle running
in perpetual abuse
torturing the reaching soul
that wants to know the good of life
but is forever battered down
into the foulness
mud and slime
dark recesses of our pain
seen somehow distant
as though on screens
of insane cinema
shown to kill
projected on our spirit
to crush away its life

so it goes
like that again
no one believes
how this can be
not even me

- Brendan Tripp
04/20/1988

LOST IN RUSHING TIME

realities swing
shifting contexts
the seeing center
is focused in and out of scene
knowing where
but not quite how
these places come to be

time is blocked
chopped up in bits
along the line
each piece is tagged
with start and end
location data
and information
fit to file
the future now

and so it goes
locked on tracks we ride
the hurtling cars of life
clacking along
the streaking rails
never stationary
never in a place
always sequential
racing forward
nearly blind

who are this people
where is this place
all is changing
as colors blur and reel
swimming vision
jumbled words
names are faceless
form lacks reason
who am I

and then break
next, the number calls
the new line enters fresh locales
altered being once again
set to hours action here
until in rushing time arrives

- Brendan Tripp
04/21/1988

IN CHAPELS OF THE FLAME

too much comes
in distant time
mind is washed
away by action
special places
focus in the light
luminescence
grips the soul
shining strangely
bringing all to change

ritual moves
within these circle bounds
fire and crystal
invade the night
vistas are unveiled
to the seeking eye
that rides the lines
of deeper inner sight
awash in color
shifting beyond form

drums sound in sanctums
of dance and chant
selves are abandoned
to meld as one
running united
into arcane plans
isolation splits
into a whole
arriving fearless
awash in light

other eyes
pierce these shadows
they set the stage
on which we play
their names are hidden
their world arcane
yet on this path
does mastery lie
just beyond
the striving of our grasp

- Brendan Tripp
04/25/1988

YET MISSING YOUR EMBRACE

almost there
and yet so far
into my darkness
you descend
to sit with me
and travel these few lines
of history preserved

is this a step
on new paths
forged in passion's wish,
or only dreams
gone false and hollow
empty in the ancient curse
within my life?

you are softness
yet do not yield
you move away
smiling at my reaches
retreating from my grasp
in subtle fading
distant and denied

shadows lurk,
the doubts and fears
of long rejected time
form a mist
a haze of inky dusk
that clouds my mind and heart
when turned to you

is this loving,
can there be love
in these shallows of my pain?
I am an ache
a craving based on you
confused and empty
not knowing where to turn

- Brendan Tripp
04/26/1988

BROUGHT FORTH AGAINST THE NIGHT

1
not enough
place in time for life
insufficient
years to craft this self
failure's curse
is the central theme
incompletion
defines what we can be

2
thoughts filter down
are sieved and exit
leaving traces
but no recall,
only echoes
spark the trailings
on their route
to unknown voids
beyond

3
vacant windows
empty eyes
blank walls shading
hollow face
broken shelter
spirits crushed
dust encroaching
tarnished dream

- Brendan Tripp
04/27/1988

RUN DOWN THROUGH EMPTY YEARS

1
old songs return
new formed

2
nothing happens
little enters
realms of linear stasis

3
isolation breaks its bonds
and seeps into the blood of life
insidiously defining
ever smaller worlds

4
going is the way
time the vital need

5
nausea inhabits
the soul, sickening,
turning rancid at the day

6
here seems a loss as central
unguided, unattached,
sent to serve the endless term
to wander in these mists

7
rage still takes its turn
causing violence to the mind

8
joy is denied
purpose drains from being
all is shadowed, hollow, grey

9
frustration is the temper of the lock
the testing of the chain
the world won't break or even bend
in pleasure or in pain

- Brendan Tripp
04/28/1988

THE FOOL AWAKES AGAIN

anguish comes again
on wings of vision
broken dreams corrupt and die
crumbling to dust
stirred by the funerary wails
that echo in this bleakest tomb
the burial plane
so nearly void
imprisoning the murdered soul
the heart so brutalized by life
the spirit ground to shattered sight
gored and empty
ripped and shredded into bits
thrown to the dogs
fed to the demons of despair...
all is lost
to love is foolish
to hope insane
and to believe the lies of goodness
or to accept
the puling propaganda of the nice
is idiocy beyond redemption
for there is nothing good in man
as love is nothing but fear of hate
and hope is nothing but delusive prayer
bent back on the weakling mind
too ready to invent a life
not damned to torment
not sentenced to eternal pain
in false mirror warpings
called the norm
where lies are truth
and the truth a dream
a nightmare screaming in the head
of hateful universes
existing to destroy
by the spawnings of a hateful race
intent on crushing out the spark
where life and love
might raise their heads
where justice and the even course
might come to form the whole anew
but all is darkness
all is damned
all is cursed to anguished life
not able to be spared

- Brendan Tripp
04/29/1988

MAY 1988

5/2/88 SMUDGED WITHIN DAY
5/3/88 THE KILLING CELL UNSEEN
5/4/88 PALE ENDINGS FOUND IN BLACK AND GREY
5/5/88 ONE SHOT AGAINST THE FLOW
5/6/88 THESE HOURS COME TOO FRAYED
5/11/88 BROKE FROM THE SIGN
5/12/88 OF ALL THESE COMING DAYS
5/13/88 DOWN INTO VALES OF DEATH
5/14/88 ATTACKING WINTER'S GREY
5/16/88 WITHIN CONCERNS OF DAY
5/17/88 NATURE OF THE SENTENCE, LIMITS OF THE CELL
5/18/88 DAMNED, CAST DOWN, DESPISED
5/19/88 FROM THE BROKEN PANE
5/20/88 BLED OUT IN USELESS DARK
5/21/88 THIS CYCLE NEARLY RUN
5/25/88 FROM UNKNOWN UNDERSTANDING SET
5/26/88 A COURSE WITHIN THE LINE
5/27/88 IN FRAGMENTARY TIME
5/29/88 BROKEN TO THESE VEILS
5/30/88 IN ROCHESTER AT DUSK
5/31/88 GROUND MINDLESS IN THESE MOMENTS' MASS

SMUDGED WITHIN DAY

sleeps stashes off these moments
thickness, heaviness
invade the senses
making all things vague
in and out of reason
we shift down from reality
and cross the ghostly line
to other places
other certainties
other worlds where to be confused
uncertain and at sea
to act out all the lives of dreams
shallow dreams
based on lines
floating off mid-sentence sense
or themed by distant TV voice
not quite shut out
not quite let in
to clearly follow
as form of data outside held
not wholly centered here
in new worlds
strangely set apart
abutting daytime
just slightly off its edge
to fallen sides of pages
hung suspended by a thread
to where we were
and who we are
not built on distant histories
that waking question
and seem too real
to be cast off as only dreams
as names return
in written time
perhaps by several days set off
but yet returned
from months and years removed
they come back
echoing from the call of dreams
splitting reason at the seams
pressing into daylight world
a fading placement
a phone line draining
of the seen

- Brendan Tripp
05/02/1988

THE KILLING CELL UNSEEN

too much wrong is
centered here
there seems malaise
at every turn
I am trapped in a capsule
of evil design
one that echoes my reach
with waves of despair
and muddles my sight
with contrary dreams
I am cut off
banished from joy
locked in dimensions
which are acid and vile
each day pulls smaller
the walls of this cell
each night rings with torment
and derisive howls
highlighting my solitude
underlining my exile
circling concepts and words in my mind
whipping into swirling miasmas of dread
seeking to retreat deeper and deeper
into the dark and silent hole
the rotten center within myself
dead, burned out by years of fiery rage
flung at all existence,
where there hangs stagnant
the stasis of the tomb
an empty stillness
a spurious peace
more akin to bones and dust
than centeredness and calm
here to hide, here to lurk
to cower against the storm outside
which seethes damnation
throughout unknowing concrete worlds
so blissfully inane
insensitive to what I see
and feel within that cutting blast
unaware of this small plane
that crushes me so deep inside
where only death can let me free
from chains that poison
the flow of life

- Brendan Tripp
05/03/1988

PALE ENDINGS FOUND IN BLACK AND GREY

darkness creeps
over absent fields
the cities
are in shadow
their buildings
shrouded in despair
deserted
void in twilight vague
winds howl
screaming half lit
unfettered cross the plane
tearing dust from sand
sand from stone
blasting structure
dimming glass
pummeling a grey
grey world
granite in light
charcoal in its shade
ebbing edges
blurring line
churning at
the dirty clouds
roiling through
disrupted skies
unwell unyielding
locking in
the secret death
the hidden plague
which lies unmoving
amid the trash
the piles of brick
and shattered steel
hid in some dark
locked down
in dimmer haze

- Brendan Tripp
05/04/1988

ONE SHOT AGAINST THE FLOW

the verbiage goes on
inside the head
racing through
the hectic swarm
of afternoons driven
against the crush of time
words run torrents
as though the dam had burst
and all the water in the world
was destined to gush through
this grey and wrinkled pass
there are lyrics
songs not quite recalled
commercial lines
and jingles of forgotten viewing
sights and books and feelings
wash up to claim their names
and submerge again
merging with the wordy flow
we try for focus
but too much is behind
pressing on
against the fragile edge
of concentration
against the brittle coat of ice
attention brings to this
it cracks as welling vision swells
into new modes
new places and new terms
not quite unnoticed
but uncaptured in its rush
associating like the net
reflective of all ones

- Brendan Tripp
05/05/1988

THESE HOURS COME TOO FRAYED

1
against the songs
of the easily inspired

again within
disjointed night

abuse of wire
within the asking

around the end
of numbers turned

almost delayed
by another's vision

2
it doesn't shift within these bounds
it fails to make its circuit
it dies in winter winds and rain
it harbors deep resentment

for there is reason quite enough
for there are forms of being
for there rise concepts on the wing
for there goes absence willing

3
strange dining
there amid the throng
two forms reach
across time
juxtaposed
side by side
the monster and the maiden
almost humorous
shift from discomfort
by weeks, by months?
it is unlined
not scripted
I hold to doubt
and settle back
to wait the waiting
wrapped in distance
and in these cares
entwined

- Brendan Tripp
05/06/1988

BROKE FROM THE SIGN

nothing enters there
nothing lives
we have the realms of empty here
we have the guns
pressed to their heads
give up the money
give up the time
all is vacant
void and blank
the wires run nowhere
all exposed like bleeding steel
still emptying the lightning blood
out on the floor
miles are walked
the linear pace
rats in mazes of deceit
that harbor promises of cheese
not given up
to colors of wrong light
the pain is piercing
to the head
the pain runs rings
into our eyes
there is no answer
only ache
we are the dying stress of time
we are a fiction
some seeming thing divorced from real
somehow apart
beyond, within the point and place
a focus burning
a straining sigh
a long extruded gasp of death
held echoing throughout all life

- Brendan Tripp
05/11/1988

OF ALL THESE COMING DAYS

what lies beyond
the motive force
outlining sight
sketching these days?

black fills boxes
cuts notches in
the calendar
of our absence

there is no theme
no purpose seen
in the going
only movement

we link to stars
on distant shores
in vain attempt
to steer new course

exotic calls
rise in the east
they draw the wing
in times of feed

can we exchange
more than these sites
can substance move
in caring ways?

down into heat
the steel is drawn
from speed to slow
reluctantly

a circle forms
to brave the hot
consuming fire
in evening's ease

some desert waits
a place of age
no telling what
may yet return

- Brendan Tripp
05/12/1988

DOWN INTO VALES OF DEATH

so much removes
reality from expectation
wishes of pleasance
always crash into disarray
and disillusion's dimming light

never does good
come into real being
only in dreams
and fantasies spun out through day
every attempt
is shattered, crushed
broken by a hostile world
thrown up by evil
in imitation of our life

it is so hard
to maintain a course of living
when every day brings new attacks
upon the soul
the heart is shredded
and decays to emptiness
which leaves a rotting aching hole
from which emotion, bleeding, flows
like acid into void
poisoning the universe
making every breath a joke
some sick jester's mime of life
more like damnation
that suicide might free

how empty are these days on earth,
how hateful, callous, is this race,
there is no goodness
there is no love
only theft, rejection, and despite,
deceit, deception, and illusion
so willingly blind
and utterly vile
it weighs upon the searching mind
that seeks a healing of the soul,
a mending of the heart,
it burns upon the eyes that see
and makes them wish for final dark,
for clearing absence gone away
to freedom, calm, and peace

- Brendan Tripp
05/13/1988

ATTACKING WINTER'S GREY

the stench of winter
clings grimy
tenacious
water does not wash
away this scent
it holds to greyness
reminder of cloud and snow
busses run through slush
and salt and wind and cold
scrub down to metal
scrub down to glass
there is springtime hidden here
somewhere beneath
these months of soot
we scour to discover warmth
the soft embrace of summer wind
so different to the blades of ice
that shredding coated
all these things
and slew the life
of sunny days before
now thickly buried
hard upon the mind
as to wrap
colors on these bars
that breezes might stir
with scent to air
again a cheery place
before the turning
of the fall

- Brendan Tripp
05/14/1988

WITHIN CONCERNS OF DAY

1
too much of softness
all around
visible it blinds the mind
so befuddled by rejection
and makes some madness
deep within
stir shudders of avoidance
which seek to flee
what it's denied

2
night's passage
brings mass to day
so new arrived
yet not so new
that it in turn turns into night
new massive night to torture day
and so a cycle
runs amok
ever upward tinged with rage

3
there is division
no flow becomes
no course is here allowed
dawn comes choppy
and way too soon to bare the eye
against the stringencies of toil
each in changed context
altered space
inverted place by days arranged

4
bases have eroded here
the foundations of false employ
crumble in the slow insistent breeze
which seeks our leaving
which bleeds in tears
of freedom long desired
not held by chains which fade in light
now breaking by some unseen sun
new risen from the haze

- Brendan Tripp
05/16/1988

NATURE OF THE SENTENCE, LIMITS OF THE CELL

stone
cement
strange encrustings
time and space
like lucite frozen
into forms
solid
stuck
illness here
badness coded
into crystal
evil etched
into this living rock
gelled from mobile time
into a picture
a diorama of the day
a joke
a cruelly sneering jest
a cycle broken
denied its growth
a needle skipping in its track
always the same
fixed
poisoned
life looped into a killing rut
that only changes names and days
but plays again
the same sick scenes
acts of torture
mind-numbing banes
again
same shit
again
new day
a helical time
a future foreknown
a sentence imposed
to damn all through life
useless life
joyless life
loveless life
denied the comforts of the race
as though the trial
had been wiped out
the memory
purged in a final scream

- Brendan Tripp
05/17/1988

DAMNED, CAST DOWN, DESPISED

darkness clutches at these eyes
even in the brightest glare of day
every scene seems distant,
artificial,
a projection set
behind some blackened screen;
and all its creatures fantasies,
cruel, sadistic phantoms
spun of spite to lure the mind
to thoughts of goodness, pleasure,
dreams of wholeness
that never are fulfilled

    I am locked
    within this hell
    I am damned
    to suffer out this life
        a sentence passed in hatred
        a torture born of flame

deep inside
the soul cries wounded,
pleading for a sudden death
aching, bleeding,
it fills the sea with rotted hopes
drained out from gashes in the heart,
foul putrescence drips from void
a gaping chasm burned from blasts
of love denied and love destroyed
and love met only with despite
in an acid, monster, evil world
that thrives upon our pain

    I am cursed
    among all men
    I am trapped
    in darkness denied light
        an empty murdered living
        a prayerless wait for death

- Brendan Tripp
05/18/1988

FROM THE BROKEN PANE

sunlight lingers
drifting warm
on diners under glass

sea creatures
walk on pavements
unnoticed with intent

input crosses time
output shifts
the way of rats is noted

afternoons fragment
in lateness arrive
pulling rugs from day

doors are open here
sequence falters
where memory resides

the gift continues
all wait payment
with sticky panting breath

erasure comes to plan
weekends spring clear
empty and uneven

trapdoors drop
bottoms empty out
anxiety eats the mind

here comes motion
with miles and thousand feet
crystal to the burn

we entice
somehow divided here
in only shade

these multitudes
rush up to fill the night
still lonely

somewhere is violence
surely being done
if only in this name

- Brendan Tripp
05/19/1988

BLED OUT IN USELESS DARK

so many place
not made transparent
the delining form
is not even lit
all harbors darkness
we and those beyond are mute
unable to relay
somehow now is stolen
from distant habit
yet even so
circles run
cutting ruts in time
carving records of frustration
insipid and useless
back and back again to things
put long before
in shadowed agony and pain
there seeks a number
or some equation's frame
for this malaise
to somehow fit the keyless lock
and break the door
allowing vision's flood to wash
away the soot and grime and filth
clung to these dungeons
these deep entrapments of the mind

- Brendan Tripp
05/20/1988

THIS CYCLE NEARLY RUN

ritual unfolds
rides down the road of time
weaving action
into webs of joined intent
interlacing days
with space and lore and truth

names come up in this
attributes of being
which in enactment
make clearing reasons why
and shift the layers
of our sight and station
changing orders
restacking the directions
of our mind
building up new towers
of these simple rough hewn blocks

texts fall out from this
strangely alter their intent
words decay
tumbling lost into some past
which seems not quite our own
we search with beams of striving
but they have somehow gone

the net is structured
and is nearly full
we await the closing of the ring
the chiming tone
to signal what has come
of all these acts
so far and yet entwined
with us and this our place
cupped in the palm of time

- Brendan Tripp
05/21/1988

FROM UNKNOWN UNDERSTANDING SET

vision comes creeping
into nights afar
improper settings
placed away from center
     perhaps this gives a breaking
     a freeing from the chains
dreamless nights and dreams
both fill as not before
as though the cycle came to close
and opened up new doors
     in low enclosure
     in bastions of the base
there with words denied
the days complete their run
and are rewarded
given open view
     somehow this seems the purpose
     the reason for our charge
secrets are fulfilled
echoing through dark
unspoken contact
links these into wholeness
     the fibers spread beyond
     reaching out to others
at first is sleep refused
agitation grips the soul
as barriers crumble
against the wave of light
     as distance fades creating one
     as names connect to vision
and then wraps darkness
cloaking, shutting out the day
pulling towards endings
frantic times of strange expulsion
     here number enters
     giving structure to desire
and dreams conclude the rite
renewed encounters
in these temples juxtaposed
seethed again within the brain
     there are sacraments
     there unveils the passage
and in the dawning
elation ensues
breaking the timeframe
to pave the crystal road

- Brendan Tripp
05/25/1988

A COURSE WITHIN THE LINE

history is not enough
it is rejected
tossed into trash cans
of our repenting
made out as dream sweat
fantasies of cultured seed
entrapped in states
of dictatorial decree
which echo down from higher courts
unyielding to our own desire
but sent to ending
set upon the chalice lip
now crumbled to the oxide snow
upon the untouched plane
unstirred, unmoving
pushed off away unheld
to breast or heart
or gory insides brought to light
eviscerations of the form
not bantered in the doctrine stream
awash in coldness
crystal shimmering in ice
that plummets from the sky
on broken wings
and symmetries unfixed
which tome to tome might wander
as empty as the night
shot down and shattered
crushed hard and sharp
outlined in brutal edges
unworded in the chants
whose low hums shake the fortress
and ring across the fields
in penitence and petition
to ask of who or where
enfolded in the wanting
the crosshairs of desire
collapsed to simple number
easy data still denied
that have their pasts yet with them
full of knowing
saddled with their time
unable to delete the chains
of reams of listed hearsay made
to run the gamut
from dust to dust again

- Brendan Tripp
05/26/1988

IN FRAGMENTARY TIME

1
there is a history
to a place like this
its walls
are noisy with it

2
the easiest way
to become old
is to begrudge another
their youth

3
dimensions number loss
the heart aches
in frustration
and anger and regret

4
anticipating boredom
set in far aways
the span extends too long
within the dreading mind

5
brackets form in time
and ask solution to their terms
here is death and childhood
here flow heat and cold

6
communications falter
in days and distance
which seek to speak
yet somehow won't suffice

7
plans set for play
come tempered
each sunny day
hides storms inside

8
all includes the lengthy list
whose ticks track down our time
enabling the clock to write
our history and life

- Brendan Tripp
05/27/1988

BROKEN TO THESE VEILS

pardon
but there is nothing
here
each frame
flashes empty
blank upon the screen
dark
void

I seek and search
but can find
no substance
no reality to feel
all a myriad swirling joke
a fantasy endured
in form of complexity
stratified

these layers
running in
endlessly
shifting
growing
rolling falsehoods into time
all unreal
all unwaking

- Brendan Tripp
05/29/1988

IN ROCHESTER AT DUSK

we walk around
and smell the waftings
of the place
seek the sizings
the lines and corners
plan and lie
feeling out this with our feet
that it be known
beyond the map
that when we go
we turn aright
and when we need
the movement comes
unthinking
one within the flow
placed within the place it is
unpanicked and a whole
     without this
     there is trouble
     denied this
     frantic feeling
     comes to rise
     enveloping the way we be
     in unsure manner
     distraction's guise
summer is around these parts
flowers call on air
across the parking lots
and streets now bare of cars
corridors wind round and round
tunnels move and twist and turn
but this is known
and filed and linked
and all is safe and good and well
in distance and aways

- Brendan Tripp
05/30/1988

GROUND MINDLESS IN THESE MOMENTS' MASS

waiting is a bruise
within these halls
seconds flagellate
in tick-tock style
the massive welts of boredom
brought down upon the mind
here the waiters do their time
like jurors corded
for some trial by fire
stacked unordered in their ranks
as though to add some extra age
to those who years have worn

this wait affects me too
as bearing down with all its mass
its sluggish seconds
its minutes taken without end
into its hours of heavy time
it crushes thought into a watch
a vigil kept for death delayed
or ending of this bided time

again the sun creeps down
the unknown heat gives way
to unfelt evening breeze
all is inside
locked away
stored against the running day's
slow motion march into the night
which only waits the scheduled dawn
to tend again the crawling clock
upon appointments
in unfixed time

- Brendan Tripp
05/31/1988

JUNE 1988

6/1/88	MUFFLED NOT WITH PLEAS
6/5/88	TUNING DRIFT, WITHIN, AWAY
6/7/88	SOMEHOW MAIMED, INVALID INSIDE
6/8/88	AGAINST INSANE DEMAND
6/9/88	BY EVENHANDED VISION SEEN
6/10/88	BLURRED BY THE TACHY RIDE
6/12/88	SO DIVIDED FROM THE STARS
6/13/88	FORMS TWISTED INTO TIME
6/14/88	NOT QUITE CAUGHT IN THE APPOINTING
6/15/88	WRONG ENTRY, WRONG INSIDE
6/16/88	THE EMPTY AND THE FEED
6/19/88	AGAINST THAT WAKING SLEEP
6/20/88	IN MASS DERIVED OF HEAT
6/21/88	BECOMING DARK AND SEEN
6/22/88	AMID THE DREAM WITHIN
6/23/88	THE PREPARATIONS FOR NO GOAL
6/24/88	FREEFALL EMPTIES OUT THE PLANE
6/26/88	LOCKED IN FRUSTRATION'S CHAINS
6/27/88	BLOCKED INTO POISONED TIMES
6/28/88	THE PLACE WE ARE WITHIN
6/29/88	TAUT WITH DIMENSION'S LIGHT

MUFFLED NOT WITH PLEAS

interference on
too many lines
garbled brainwaves
define the place
the time
edginess answers
the telephone ring
as eyes dart jumpy
impossible to control
     here we are
     bored to tears
     beset by nerves
     amid these fears
or something
like that
enticing to the letter form
the structured mass
the elephant not born by lies
fed by too many words
     in circles too small
     yet constantly defined
     in patterns unseen
     lurking still in the mind
there it goes
the feedback loop
all as in enters out
muted voices scream the silence
not in the ear
buried backwards in the brain
walled up in cages
not to be seen
until that dying day

- Brendan Tripp
06/01/1988

TUNING DRIFT, WITHIN, AWAY

this is the part
the part
I really hate,
the void
the blankness

     and cracks appear
     ripped through spacetime
     like arrows jetted
     against a win that dies
     bleeding out tomorrow's form

all useless
exiled to afar
points too distant
unable to tap those spirits
where inspiration comes

     fabrics turn and fold
     in dimensions not graspable
     ripples flow to eddies
     and then to crushing waves
     heralding the change

this is broken
a receiver stuck
on stations not attuned
knowing faintly off the band
in static drowned

     there comes passage then
     open to these future pasts
     where pens rewrite the history
     and shuttle anguish into dark
     some million count away

- Brendan Tripp
06/05/1988

SOMEHOW MAIMED, INVALID INSIDE

1
insufficient answers
come to mind
unsatisfactory solutions
are applied
     the whip of change
     cracks turbulence to life
     in pressing on the run of days
2
searching is aborted
somehow priorities
realign, shift the order
make strange the view of time
as though the switches threw
tracks into different space
     some altered where
     that holds the promise
     one time made
3
difficulties arise
like creeping waters
of melting poles
slowly taking unawares
the sleeping village by the shore
     stealthily it steals the land
     and rips away the blocks of day
     so central to the mark of time
4
tongue-tied confusion
envelops the mind
spun between the wall of plenty
and the void of empty life
     reality has its focus lost
     its framings now decay
     into chaos and the fade
5
central to the need is want
basic to its structure, names
not given, not allowed
like lightning caught by accident
not captured by intending eyes
or given to take home
     pretty crystal playthings all
     whose sharp sharp edges
     still cut us to the very quick

- Brendan Tripp
06/07/1988

AGAINST INSANE DEMAND

there evolves a clashing
of wills and time
jostling schedules
to fit the tight surrounds
of hours spent within
these narrow walls
these realms of little minds

and from this violence
a friction builds
which heats the spirit
by the incessant chafe
of dictates against nature
that try to crush
the truer self inside

a conflagration builds
from these contrary sparks
that strike the waiting tinder
of hatred and its rage
to light again
those dreadful flaming depths
long buried in the soul

when cycles are returned
to anger's ways again
there disillusion
cast shadows upon life
forming darkness
which clouds our vision
with thoughts of uselessness and death

and in this midnight
this blackness hot with hate
we seek that killing
the blow that would collapse the world
and tear away the walls
of enslaved being
thus unbinding captive time

- Brendan Tripp
06/08/1988

BY EVENHANDED VISION SEEN

1
there falls, these fall
plummeting from some tawdry height
tarnished in the light of want
unbalanced by the pressing wind
to circle spirals ever down
in dimensions of a space denied
not handled by the arcane night
spun out by chemically laced dreams

2
we seek the conflict
charge out to find
the challenge of our mail
which gleams through darkness
and shines against the empty black

3
years have elapsed before
this return is exercised
towards those nearer realms
     with new faces peopled
     with new rules decreed
it slices up the evening time
already chopped to artful bits
allowing that the whole be made
beyond the scope of all the parts
     for knowing, going
     for absence not abstained

4
strain against internal stress
as pressure builds
lateral force on linear fault
nearing blackout to align
the preferred order
the ordinated form

5
and so, homecomings are set
in times to come anon
we cloak the ebon shade
and move deeply in the past
reciting mantras of our youth
strange shadows in a future dark
led into memory

- Brendan Tripp
06/09/1988

BLURRED BY THE TACHY RIDE

sight of motion
racing within the head
hurtling past phrases
visions built of sound and light
not quite whole
cloaked in darkness like the screen
untriggered status
unset locus of the stream
flashing towards some central point
vanishing in infinities
all is speed
and motive pressings into states
made more like violence
tactilely banking through these turns
with observing eyes within
almost ripping from the skin
into some new dimension's arms
grey like pages moved too fast
bent in light twisted
funnel mirrors presentation
rattling the now spewing text
against the twitching mind
as all slides past
and numbers rotate ever up
gauges toting up the marks
of strange attainment
and measurements still undefined
dashing into future lines
in consecrations of the past
culled from rituals of need
the ebbing currents of the word
within the backwash of our life
that billows in its myriad forms
of cloud and foam and smoke and steam
and then shoot by
tearing somehow at the head
spinning consciousness to set
in focus on the tunnel seen
with accelerating drive
streaming, blurring
into indistinction
uncatchable, untamed

- Brendan Tripp
06/10/1988

SO DIVIDED FROM THE STARS

1
from there issues
no tremors
amid these very few
the swirl of power does not appear
the date, the numbers
these seem aright
yet absence enters
at the very root
sending the seekers
disappointed into darkness
into void

2
ease comes to meetings
near to matchings
so divorced from set
patterns of behavior
the normal stupid course of day
locked into its sad return
this leaving changes all
and makes the self less vile
less grotesque
when shown the mirror of man
so that fellowship and trust
might hint their will to be

3
the flow seems broken
into chunks and shards
divided bits
each to its own time space
apart like skits
in incoherent theater
strung without a central theme
into some life
some masquerade of being
     from tragedy to panic
     from joy to peace it jerks
     each one a whole
     each one a world
unfitted to a reason
to pattern unsustained
this becomes a fate
a jagged limbo of existence

4
spans leave off
and wait for change
questions form of time
and doubt arrives
again to plague the calm
that seeks the difference
that strives to free
and to be free
    we see the walls
    invisible
    we touch the bars and ask
    "how long for me"
    how long we wonder
    that this bondage be made
    our onerous yoke
    our millstone dragging down
    from reaches
    that these visions show to be
    our right
    and growth that should soon be
    our destiny
    our heritage attained

- Brendan Tripp
06/12/1988

FORMS TWISTED INTO TIME

we go up
and are unawares
taking clouds by storm
unstorming in the baking heat
of summer's wrath misplaced
     to cut through mists
     with swords of eyes
seeking out the landmarks
that may define the texture
of the places
made common through our days

these attributes
can not escape
yet slipping they still fade
off to questions, indistinct
     vague like sleeping
     dull in stupid time
they churn the names
and tear the heart to shreds
not knowing what the distance brings
but for hope and tears

overloaded mind
groans under data's mass
too much has now been seen
too many places ventured
     a haze hangs upon us
     thick with pulling tides
the mouth is set agape
unable to define
the basic state
to output existential whys

pencils mark
divisions to our being
creating doctrine
delineating time
     dream within dreaming
     echoes age to death
the bonds are growing tighter now
they cut the flow of life
as spirit gasps for open air
and soul prepares to fly

- Brendan Tripp
06/13/1988

NOT QUITE CAUGHT IN THE APPOINTING

the intention
has taken too far back
strength is seen within decay
reordered to be nameless
as calls on wires
reshuffle doubt
and put aside the blade of ending
long prepared among the files
in waves of nauseating hope
     foolish thought
     to trust in time
to feel a healing might ensue
of all these battered scars

smiles come breaking
out of mists
cloaked behind our ignorance
and hint of planning,
discussions of conspiracy
that we know not about;
a change is feared,
our vectors may be wrong
and steerage on false heading
     as shifted poles may bring
     new unsuspected stars
yet blithely we advance to ends
that have not been foreseen

there are answers
to qualitative sets
there are ways of growth
within this heat
the rotation of cycles
erupts from our grave
and sprays the world with iron and chain
framed by time and chatter
and enumerated more
     what is given is desired
     dear to night's embrace
there are patterns to this call
that allow our thoughts to spin

- Brendan Tripp
06/14/1988

WRONG ENTRY, WRONG INSIDE

dawn abruptly cuts the night
and enters to the palace
dark hallways beckon with their age
towards secrets in the murk
this is the seat of the abyss
its massive pull rings from the walls
     its presence everywhere
     within the keep is felt

scratches have abused the sheen
of marble and the polished stone
smooth surface marred with warning signs
the dying words of those before
etched for the ages
mute screams against our step
     here never to be heard
     and never to be seen

somewhere behind the ears
now floats a tune's vague line
familiar, calling to the mind
beyond location
somehow set off as in the soul
not placed or truly grasped
     whose action plays this reed
     that ushers us inside?

the patterns on the floor
erupt to number too correct
and stun perception's sight
all aspects fall into their place
as though again a trap had sprung
within the master plan
     new darkness folds across
     a morn too briefly light

- Brendan Tripp
06/15/1988

THE EMPTY AND THE FEED

from deep inside
the crawling comes
an itch that reaches
from the gut
and rakes nails at the mind
which tries to shun
the strong demand
and cycles through
the reasons why
there is no feeding
no sustenance supplied

but it won't stop
each moment turns again within
no other topic is allowed
focus bounces
from what needs be
to the ache
the void within
it scuttles thinking
and makes for stupid glassy stares
which rate the world
in terms of food

temptation nibbles
around the edges of the will
gnawing at determination
to beat the urge to eat
weakness swirls a ripple
through the middle of the soul
and turns to crumbs
the fixed idea
of diet and control
somewhere between the cracked intent
and the open larder's door

- Brendan Tripp
06/16/1988

AGAINST THAT WAKING SLEEP

dark doors open
unintended
probes of vision
pierce awareness
as weighty clouds
usher in
a sleep of color
a thickness stealing
volition from the mind
shrouding heavy sheets
around the greater form
cocooning in a mummy wrap
for unasked journeys
the floating self

here are new things given
against the old
all tinged with terror
unfamiliar
we fight the grip
to struggle back
to waking states
and linear time
yet this waits lurking
in wrinkles in the grey
to drag us into
these other realms
when unsuspecting we relax
the watch upon the real

- Brendan Tripp
06/19/1988

IN MASS DERIVED OF HEAT

dry comes the heat
and echoes of the future place
folded in return
days now past and days to come
we greet them
spreading knowledge
offering the mode to be
sending into vectored night
the distant spans' locale
this is the seeding
the open oven door
set in skies to desiccate
the dusty land
pouring sweat from fainting brows
on the trail of common ease
now straining at the task
wondering what comes
in long day walkings
new journeys we will make
in the sere and powdered ground
baked solid in the sun
as so we sleep
or try to sleep
and live until the dark
streaming precious water lost
to ever thirsty air
hiding for the ritual
unspoken and unsure
anticipating what might be
under the canopy of stars
cut by winds uncaring
not knowing what these are
or of ourselves
what names we have
pronounceable by night
there is a sullen thickness here
a mass built of the heat
which grips the avenues
of midday concrete motion
and makes all going slow
defying the equating mind
to define its lines of grasp
the bends and folds
now grow complex
as time shuttles in between
the simmer and the fade

- Brendan Tripp
06/20/1988

BECOMING DARK AND SEEN

split to sultry dreams
of porous sad perception
schism like the death
that lets return
to modes of life
and enter into shadow realms
to see what needs be seen
all has slid
down along that way
the slippery slide
which beckons to that place
we can not hold
to these views of the real
nor can we stay
in vistas safe for man

thus does the chasm
gape large before our path
and promises destruction
if not its will obey
as every step
shifts rocks into its maw
not too far off
focus runs to miniscule
the tiny grindings
dividing us from plummet
and the fall

inversion strikes
somehow the inside runs to out
and we are new yet old
staring with the unright eye
at the ruin of the world
made pointless by the seeing
and useless by the known
tools of futures come to bear
from put off states retrieved
as isolation is controlled
to slave the flying time
in manners given of the east
and opened to the mind
as yet unsettled
and demon wracked
swathed with the thickness
the weight and mass
awaiting now to hatch

- Brendan Tripp
06/21/1988

AMID THE DREAM WITHIN

1
the animals gather round
to partake them of this nectar
there is dance
in shadow realm

lo, these calls come down the decades
and echo with the night
we are compelled
into this action

beneath the surface lurks truth
a sweeping clears away this dust
there now rings
the chimes aright

2
the mountain
resounds with hidden light
it pulls me back
to its embrace
I hear its hum
within my soul

gleaming crystal peak
unseen but in these dreams
stabs brilliance to my skull
leaves me stunned
shook and empty
glowing with its shine

3
the body is taken
into the dance
uncontrolled

this song comes unasked
to fly on wings
all its own

the gateway unlocks
by moving mists'
vibration

our anguish ensues
from the shifting
into strength

4
bear straight the central course ahead
the narrow path flanked by the dead

be mindful of the grueling test
which takes the weak yet spares the best

across that chasm deep and wide
be focused whole on every stride

in knowing fail not certainty
still guided by humility

embrace the power in the clouds
obtaining all that is allowed

carve out your niche within the sky
by tasting death before you die

5
who is sacrificed
amid the growing light
and scattered time
who has answered calls
made aeons in the past
to see these ways
and know these things
so different from their world
and its logic
who encompasses
the heart of fire and holds
the distant stars

- Brendan Tripp
06/22/1988

THE PREPARATIONS FOR NO GOAL

a grid appears
from nowhere
lays down lines
for no good use
and taunts
as though these passings
are as useless as
the heart would fear

too many things
demand our time
they batter at the door
of mind and focus
and insist
to option off our now
devoid of plan
and all derailed

so sheets fly
from calendars
in time delay effect
black and white cliché
each twists
the tension cord
each makes the worry
more intense

other dictates run
against the day
we have no version
to display
no doctrine
to scream at crowds
just motion cranking
into that void

these vectors spread
from indecision
like collider spawn
across the gel
they tear intent
down into fragments
forming halts
doldrums and decay

- Brendan Tripp
06/23/1988

FREEFALL EMPTIES OUT THE PLANE

and suddenly
the platforms falter
support erodes
flow is strangled
making arid
these frozen wastes
     terror swells
     a tremor undermining
     the place we stand
     all is shadowed in the light
     gripped by illness
     and driven by the panic whip
          attempt retreat
          the mode of shut down
          switches thrown
          and all the levers tried
          to cease the cycle
          to break the hold on thought

there it goes
again

entering the absent ways
built up of silent fear
locked into the insane day
and washed by seas of tears

     broke down by blows of blindness
     in the madhouse of the sane
     denied the slightest kindness
     and unjustly thrown in chains

enveloped in this vision
awakened to this eye
how cruel this mundane prison
in which they'd see me die

and so involves
     guesswork
     forming reason
          corrupting
crystals form of seed
     in solution
          not solved
     unscheduled
     disengaged

- Brendan Tripp
06/24/1988

LOCKED IN FRUSTRATION'S CHAINS

that dividing
heats rage
which breaks apart
the logic flow
and interrupts
the mind
making priorities
of frustration
of anger
    silent screams
    that barely keep their peace
    in irritation
    hostility towards the world
    that taunting world
    which shadows out of reach
    as though through mirrors
    into reflections
    of other places yet denied,
    joys and pleasures
    forever kept away
here alien
the fool
stupid puppet
of their despite
a prisoner
encaged
in wall-less cells enchained
for this torture
forever

- Brendan Tripp
06/26/1988

BLOCKED INTO POISONED TIMES

1
wrong place
wrong time
plunk
     concrete reality
shatter
     the skull
     is split asunder
shake
     spasms control
     the death throe
     psychic dance
where is escape
where were the exits
on this plane?
          steel on steel
          grinding
          there is no release
          the belts they are alive
          and hostile
          they grip us to our seats
          and grin
          making certain
          we stay through movies
          endure the ride

2
the inside is
unwell
stripped of armor
it is naked
bleeding and exposed
shelter has no home for this
we are disposed
scourged and exiled off to die
in acid wastes beyond the wall
     why are we flotsam,
     why thrown from crystal palace here?
anguish pulses
through our veins,
we taste the dusts
of poisoned land
as winds rip grit against our bleeding hides
and drives us to our knees in pain,
hunched and dying,
torn by loathing of our state
beyond the outside
thrown down to ashes
this emptiness of guilt and shame
now cradle to our bones

3
there come divisions
ranks aligned within the world
to cast the mettle
steel the very stuff of self
     these now I spy
     as in some distance
     cloaked by haze
     or back behind some swirling glass
     which cuts me from that focus
far off the drumming
now can be heard
as all the armies gird for war
and don the mantle of new madness
     insane, I too
     cower in my corner
     not knowing how
     these visions will effect my fate
     so absent and removed
"away with mind"
they scream in blood lust
"and let the faithful take the day"
to arms and to the fray
     they can not see
     they play the same part
     each foe himself
     is scripted as the enemy
     identically cast

4
the little deaths
well up inside
places dying
within the soul
bit by bit are
turned to ashes
the casualties
of wasted days
formed in old dread
and fed on greed
unholy way
to bide ones time
this dying life
awaits the grave
and looks to dark
for its release
a chance to flee
to peaceful void
free of those chains
forged by the day

- Brendan Tripp
06/27/1988

THIS PLACE WE ARE WITHIN

stress pulls pain
across the chest
panic changes air
into some broth
thickly poisoned
made crazy
green and brown
tinged with rot
swirling all around
screams insist
break bolts through fog
shatter focus
erupt in mind
more pain stabs
within the gut
all is ache
malaise and dread
volume sizzles
alive with malice
all electric
ready to shock
there are no outs
no way to safety
the universe
is all one blade
sharpness set to cut
to plunge and pierce
to dice, destroy
to tighten bands
sprouting spikes
ever inward
shooting pain
making panic
all mirrored with rage
killing locus
unhealthy space
acid dripping
faulty air
spinning cruelly
hateful space
making being
wish to die

- Brendan Tripp
06/28/1988

TAUT WITH DIMENSION'S LIGHT

1
for there becomes this void
tense with anticipation
manic in its shifting dark
virtual worlds express
apprehension in perception
so close to being's threshold
that flight is almost palpable
in proximity to here

2
sheets of steel
come crashing out of time
as if to close
these elements of day
into sectors
divisions of our lives

3
we reach
and so extend
beyond the place
of now
we hurry
beyond the moment
to attain
some phantom
some wisp of futures
forever beyond
our rushing grasp

4
still deep within
there are eyes, calm,
subtle, seeing
truth and only
things of the true;
there is center
there lurks the soul
in cool quiet
distant, constant
in sad repose
waiting ever
for our return

- Brendan Tripp
06/29/1988

JULY 1988

7/1/88 THE STATIONS OF OUR DOOM

7/5/88 IN THE SHALLOWS OF REGRET

7/6/88 THE CENTER ROTTED, THE WORLD DECAYED

7/7/88 UP TOWARDS THE EDGE OF WISDOM

7/8/88 A SHIFT TO CHAIN AND DISTANCE

7/11/88 DEPRESSION'S GRASP FORMS DYING

7/12/88 TRANSMUTATION'S ALCHEMY

7/13/88 PRISONER TO A SUICIDAL LIFE

7/14/88 YET LOCKED WITHIN THIS HELLISH PLACE

7/15/88 AN INDEX OF THE HEAT

7/17/88 THESE SHADOWS GATHER, SUICIDAL

7/18/88 RODE THROUGH STORM, THROUGH HEAT

7/19/88 THE PULSE THAT SOUNDS WITHIN

7/20/88 WHAT'S GONE AND WHAT'S DENIED

7/21/88 WITHIN THESE WINGS, AWAITING TIME

7/22/88 THE BLOOD OF DARKNESS, THE BILE OF LIGHT

7/25/88 VISTAS FROM THIS PLACE

7/26/88 THE BLADES OF LIFE DISSECTING

7/27/88 PEELING THROUGH THE VEILS OF SELF

7/28/88 FOUND IN SPACE UNMARKED

7/29/88 IN CANYON DEPTHS, BEYOND

THE STATIONS OF OUR DOOM

1
anguish enfolds
the anniversary day
in the manners of its
creation

2
time becomes liquid
across these years
and banishes joy
to memory

3
exiled like carriers
of the plague
I am turned from the gates
that should be mine

4
deep within
hate's cauldron boils
searing all to twisted form
and warping beams of sight

5
I am unknown
existing but in rumor
to fade like legends
in old minds

6
newness breaks out
into sorrowful worlds
fresh cycles of blindness
have thus begun

7
these are the doldrums
the shallows of being
we sit becalmed
to starve and to die

8
no knife appears
at killing stones
where we have thrown
our sacrifice

9
this purgatory
seems confused
mixed with breath it lives
mocking truthful life

10
I wring my hands
and wish my heart would burst
so burdened by
this pointless being

11
a pall hangs over sunlight
a shroud now veils the day
this is a dream
emitting from the tomb

12
all things fade
but seldom die
there bleeds an empty
long before the void

- Brendan Tripp
07/01/1988

IN THE SHALLOWS OF REGRET

sad sweet sorrow
clings to the fibers
of my soul
puts soft chains
around my heart
and drags me down
to puddles of remembrance
the mirroring ponds
of what has been
glinting subtle evening light
into patterns
forming mights and coulds
wistful musings
of how some other life would sound
without the weighing
of this heavy self

it seems all lost
gone to emptiness and shame
poisoned failings
wrenched from promise and denied
access to beauty,
a way to truly feel
the springs of joy,
a path to touch
the pretty things within the world
that we now scarcely see
and can not know
what pleasures they entail

in so much going
there is barely one arrived
the self hangs distant
suspended by the damning bonds
at far remove from human worlds
let only to strain
to see the actions
of that life
only to wish
for an active realer form
to make existence whole
and so to walk
upon that stage
in blindness of the actors part
united with mere fate
and full within that guise of life

- Brendan Tripp
07/05/1988

THE CENTER ROTTED, THE WORLD DECAYED

more analgesics are imported
into the den of pain
given the impossibility of escape
and the likelihood
of death in chains
slaved into pointless loiterings
made in the guise of clocks
wishing for the edit
breaking from the age
as if those years were just erased
and more pleasant scenes
scribbled in their stead
to make the story nicer still
stripped of sickness
cleansed of the seeds of rage
purged of hateful loneliness
and the fires within the mind
that have tempered every thought
with the warping force of anger
so that isolation
becomes the only cool retreat
exiled to ice
dragged off wounded to cold caves
where goodness shatters
frozen in the air
that blows from voids once seat to souls
which died from contact with the world
in the charring heat of the expulsion
when we were damned to this decay
becalmed and waiting
biding on a change
or counting down to death;
how unpleasant is this life
how useless breathing in this shell
which moves though being
and the embodied modes
yet can not touch the essences
of what it sees around;
yes, there is darkness welling here
a tide of breaking surge
which is felt in distant ways
moving in the final reach
of mismatched worlds at odds
soon crashing into violence
to wield destruction
so desperately desired

- Brendan Tripp
07/06/1988

UP TOWARDS THE EDGE OF WISDOM

I didn't know
I had a future
as it emptied into time
I didn't see
the web unwinding
at the tolling of the chime
I didn't feel
the past's long shadow
as it echoed ancient rhyme
I didn't guess
that there was something
beyond living life in mime

we are exiled
into this darkness
for our searing crimes of hate
we are cast down
upon the planet
and now know of it too late
we are detained
apart from wholeness
and so bitter is our fate
we are shackled
onto misery
and are hung with living's weight

there are visions
that now come to me
which have spoken of the sky
there are colors
pulsing through the mind
never tasted by the eye
there are voices
heard within the night
that are echoes to our cries
there are reasons
hidden in the world
which explain the way we die

- Brendan Tripp
07/07/1988

A SHIFT TO CHAIN AND DISTANCE

these do not work
within available absence
they run too long
and hurt the brain
I cut
I delete
and make blank again the screen
as pulses ebb
somewhere inside the head
I reach for medication
to attenuate the pain
nearly empty
nearly gone
there is intent
for the refill
we here are crippled
yet throw away
the crutch of rhyme
allowing time instead
to seep into these places
and force the touch
of planes within the gap
for the instant
I am here
we have contact
but then again the base
gives way to sliding
as though the floor had dropped
and opened onto chutes
into memory
echoing what was
as basis of will-be's
as processors take up
their sorting task
and wrap
the seeing self
within the data flow
     where are
     we within this time
     where are
     the guideposts of position
again there comes the lost
thrown into corners never real
to wallow and to cry
in broken states
of hollowness and pain

- Brendan Tripp
07/08/1988

DEPRESSION'S GRASP FORMS DYING

waves of depression hit
a dense fog of demoralization
sweeps in around the soul
and makes life seem a cage
every error blows up huge
and mocks existence
taunting our inadequacies
as all our failings grow
to massive stature of defeats
shadowing the world in dark
an acid shade that eats the mind
and strips away what shreds of pride
that might have clung
to stupid self
from paltry pointless past success
accomplishments seen now as dust
useless ashes held in ignorance
to be of value

and now so low
we see ourselves as worthlessness
worthy only of the slime
or of the graveyard, put away,
dropped from realms in which we fail
discarded into all that's vile
disgusting self, worthless I,
putrid being of the depths
striving for the will to die
to kill the self
to so destroy
the pointless torture of this life
ground into isolation's grip
cut off forever
from blessings, joy, and smiles
to only hope for icy void
and empty endlessness unknowing
how far debased existence was

- Brendan Tripp
07/11/1988

TRANSMUTATION'S ALCHEMY

drop and
fall to places
of the dark
given tunes
never lines
with arcane names
unspoken
hidden
tucked within
the folds of time
well away
from sight and reason
these are the entrance
to the temple
ancient halls
massive columns
so aligned
long into
the distant space
bright light
cutting, aching
piercing from the throne
trumpets blare
a world's vibration
shaking down
the very bone
tearing out
the mind and will
melting being
into sand
cut into pieces
pulsed by unheard beat
and returned
to realms of dark
cloaked in velvet
bagged to void
shattered fragments
held gleaming
precious for the feast
taken in winds
bent before the field
and freed
into wordless realms
new dimensions
opened but by death
to be seen

\- Brendan Tripp
07/12/1988

PRISONER TO A SUICIDAL LIFE

great blankness envelops,
pressing downward on the stars,
flattening the world outside
and causing the decay
of the will to live
     how to frame
     this depression?
     how to put
     words to this malaise?
every act
seems useless in this light
every thought
is echoed by emotion's wails
     to do is pointless
     to be is a defeat
these eyes have become privy
to the grain within the world
they see the tiny fragments
which build by blurring
into the structures given sense
     and form the universe
     agreed upon by man
and in this sight
each element seems huge
each item grabs attention
and we are pulled
from point to point
in frantic need to act
     but these are infinite
     and can not be sustained
and thus frustration
locks claws into the soul
halting motion
creating death in life
     we know no relief
     we do not trust the lies
blackness reaches from within
to crush the hope of good
there is no winning in the world
there are no truths to know
all is poisoned, vile and sick,
soaked in acid which destroys
the heart, the mind, and soul
     chained into being
     deprived of death
     held hostage by the act of life

- Brendan Tripp
07/13/1988

YET LOCKED WITHIN THIS HELLISH PLACE

these memories
glimpses of freedom
snatched by night
beyond the cage
     in these soaring
     becomes the mode
     in these new worlds
     open to the eye

bitterness fills up
the heart is acid
and cries on shackles
hard upon the hands
     all things unpleasant
     here
     all days destructive
     now

how could the sentence
give way to light
and let those words
well up from singing soul?
     somewhere within
     there is a point of joy
     somewhere inside
     there still is fervent hope

disillusionment tinges
mind in emotion's pain
all is conspiring
to form a world of hate
     dreams blend with vision
     to cloud the view of time
     dreams fall to prayer
     to be delivered from this chain

scarred self stands lonely
and stares into the dark
treacherous are the roads
that lead off from this place
     can there be releasing
     from the agony of life?
     can there come supplanting
     of this endless nightmare's reign?

- Brendan Tripp
07/14/1988

AN INDEX OF THE HEAT

boiling
heat surrounds
humidity
denies relief
as sweat pours
rivers down
steaming skin
heat index
counts the rise
swelling
numbers run
to hazard
one hundred
and twenty
dangerous day
with no air left
to evaporate
perspiring wet
at forty five
percent
thick humid air
even breeze
just moves hot gas
no relieving
draining curtain
one by one
machines now fail
struggling
against the press
of stewing atmosphere
they too heat
as overdriving
circuits die
faltering
in massive pulls
on power centers
burned a hundred high
without a cloud
without a prayer
dripping moisture
poached by sun
in massive, crushing
summer air

- Brendan Tripp
07/15/1988

THESE SHADOWS GATHER, SUICIDAL

so little reason
can be seen
to justify existence;
there seems no point
to living,
there is no good
in futures
built on bases of today

I yearn for dying,
I ache for darkness and release;
I see myself
and see but error,
wrongness, badness,
corruption and decay

I stand alone
denied all contact,
unable to reach out for aid;
there is no care
for me in living,
no softness, comfort, or relief,
only anger, alienation,
coldness, distance and despite
greet my waking eyes
and torment me
in realms of sleep

these days come hard
and wracked with anguish
as my soul searches
for some escape,
a last gasp effort
to find some reason
to live, to be,
to sentence self
to still exist

- Brendan Tripp
07/17/1988

RODE THROUGH STORM, THROUGH HEAT

rain hits the city
cleans the streets
curtains the buildings
in sheets of grey
soaking with camo stripes
of wet and dry cement

     busses drive through
     the summer storm heat
     their escape windows open
     to let in the air
     this ventilation
     gives access to rain

     streaming down panes
     dripping from cracks
     water runs inside
     it fills half the seats,
     like birdbaths on wheels
     bowls sloshing along through the ride

the summer is long
locked in drought
these downpours are welcome
to settle the dust
shift grass to green
and sweeten the air

- Brendan Tripp
07/18/1988

THE PULSE THAT SOUNDS WITHIN

these musics
run within me
I am audience
to the once-heard sound
that leaves a fading ripple
within my head

somewhere inside
there are echoes,
sympathetic ringings
long buried in the depths
of these songs and words,
vibrations that strive
to surface in the world
somehow kept off
on other planes
across some membrane felt
as distant pining
for their release

disjointed feelings
accompany the song
as though the singer
and I are somehow one
divided but by time and space
yet not in truth apart

at night sometimes
when inner seas are tossed
from mania to depression
and back again
this mirroring can be seen
the troughs of missing
give way to crests
of unity with beat
and pulse driven to the word
wrapped frantic in expression
only to slip once more
into convention's now

there is a sense of steel
made crystal in the night
of what there is
and what should be
of who and what I am
and what is really me

- Brendan Tripp
07/19/1988

WHAT'S GONE AND WHAT'S DENIED

the past shudders
fast and furious
echoes up the ages
to make black and white
these papers speak nothing
mean nothing
only ink
only clinging carbon
useless without lexicon
blank as though the page were empty
void of meaning
screaming in a taunting rage
at all our ignorance
the knowing we do not
and minds that aren't possessed
of these essentials
these meaning that we need
to form the concept
to open up the door to light
and let the matrix
form in thought
some crystal structure
myriad in its gleaming way
fascinating
drawing focus deep within
into itself
into its being
pulling into realms of color
glittering color
frosted light
where time decays
and drops off empty
a useless husk of yesterday
denied this crystal
denied connection
the shining links within the form
built of the knowing
born of the concept
run through the channels
of mental function we so lack
here in our darkness
here stuck in time
in chains of space and reason
as much of ashes
gone down to nothing
as is our past

- Brendan Tripp
07/20/1988

WITHIN THESE WINGS, AWAITING TIME

whence issues pain
from here
from heaven sent
from depths of hell
made present in our world
to crack temporal spans
with fissures of anguish
unattained within desire
unmatched by backgrounds
detailed by sad refrains
of wailing masses
locked into their wheels
of turning cycles
impossible and unseen
flames reach higher
passing levels of the greater world
scorching through the planes of life
to lick at battlements
bastions of the highest state
as though to scream
petitioning our release
from unjust chaining
in lower realms

here is recoil
and stagger back from open scenes
rife with sores of vision
plaited through the strands of time
a tapestry demanding depth
and total distance so to read
the meaning of its weave
splayed through the darkness
hung in the universal void
which clasps the galaxies of stars
as in a setting strung with light
a bauble cherished, hid away
from those eyes tortured
in the turning flames of cycled being
in the rut of round and round
the chain of racing existence run
forever locked in pain
from this
from nothing formed
from absent self
made seeming in our world
and shadowed by that sense of I

\- Brendan Tripp
07/21/1988

THE BLOOD OF DARKNESS, THE BILE OF LIGHT

dig down deep
through the hours
and excavate
the ashes of the day:
     here lie the secrets
     and the patterns
     lost to life,
     broken pieces
     of intention,
     and fragments
     of these shattered hopes
     strewn in layers
     defying plan

(hollow chambers
wait below,
the void of anguish
denied all time)

futility
builds up its marks
describing platforms
of the pyre
     there are reasons
     somewhere within,
     purpose hiding
     beyond some distant wall
the tribe is marching
to this place,
the sacrifice
can now be made
     and lo, the die is cast,
     the victim chosen
     as in a nightmare
     always self

(this knowing
does the one no good;
no paths are open,
no actions are sustained)

          Here comes seeing
          borne on night
          here arrives
          the virtue bearing
          all within the dark...

- Brendan Tripp
07/22/1988

VISTAS FROM THIS PLACE

1
broken image comes
across days too short
erasing mind
clearing places
new within the void
2
the network balks
the lacings falter
faced with lists too long
there is no doing
no manner of display
3
are gaps not there
enumerated?
we count these things
to know our state
and yet dumbfounded stand
4
a strain runs into time
stresses at the week
makes our focus fracture
how can these lives
be still the same?
5
we know this going
will be distraught
we know the place
will not be taken
by presence of the self
6
from sky does noise
descend on man
erupting in attention
crumbled with seeing
shattered with speed
7
no use, the spans
expand and shrink
in opposition's way
we are unsettled,
blocked and all denied

- Brendan Tripp
07/25/1988

THE BLADES OF LIFE DISSECTING

entirely deserted
soul opens up and bleeds
the black flow of emotion
gushing from the wound of life
spilling torrents on the world
which bears the piercing edge
penetrating unto death

placed into smaller spaces
the universe falls down
and suffocates the self
    there is no freeing
    no escape
as centered in a neutron star
all is mass and locked in time
where freedom is a myth
and panic is the pulse of life
running ragged the mobile mind
into cycles of retreat,
frantic, fleeing everything

    can death be any worse
    than this masquerade of life?

cessation of being
always tempts
the battered, broken soul
thoughts of void
ring cool and sweet
against the misshapen form of day
    so clearly wrong
    so hateful, vile
there is no leaving
and all is chain

time transmutes
to crushing mass
that twists the mind
in agony and torment
and makes the seeing point cry out
to slide back into darkness
regretting that it came to be
within the killing world

    what purpose leads selfhood
    to justify this anguish?

- Brendan Tripp
07/26/1988

PEELING THROUGH THE VEILS OF SELF

what runs through
the mind
scraps of stuff
picked up here and there
tunes and words
pulled from stories
newspapers, magazines
and these books
we always read
forming images and swirls
in kaleidoscopic sound
     this is the upper level
     the flow of data
     like a text

also there runs through
the self
a different line
this is flavored
with emotion's taint
and speaks of panic
anxiety and fear
it is built
of strangled hopes,
love shattered on the rocks
of crumbled aspirations
     this is the middle level
     the flow of anguish
     like lost blood

sometimes this runs through
the gut
a pulse, a charge,
a gripping press of speed
which kicks to mania
and opens up
those other states
which have been too long estranged
cloaked by acid tinged with dread
blocked from being
in the world
     this is the central level
     the flow of passion
     like hot wires

- Brendan Tripp
07/27/1988

FOUND IN SPACE UNMARKED

before the transferal
duration shifts
becomes unstatic
flips like files and not a flow
like slides on one projector
giving way to blanks between
flashing with the moment's gaze
of attention
focused into glare

there are not
the words allowed
because of when
the going is

all the lists are checked and done
enumerated with the mind
to not let slip the opportune
window of becoming
still resistance claws within
and slows the actions of the course
not into being
not broken space
the elements of wheres we see

disallowed then
become old ways
swept beyond
the clouds and sky

here scuttled vision
decays the trace
as memories erupt
in exposition of the day
there are the functions
brought down by choice
hollow motions run to dreams
which betokened spread the lore
of absences deserving night

hand the vacant
pass the blank
worlds have perished
to be reborn

- Brendan Tripp
07/28/1988

IN CANYON DEPTHS, BEYOND

darkness falls
warming sunlight creeps away
up these cliffs
as greyness settles on the canyon
where dead cities cling to walls
in distance like cartoons
small, like toys,
fragile and unreal

quiet hollow,
this place seems built by time
and speaks of ages hid away
in ancient walls
and stone that shatters from some sea
a million years removed,
its only sounds are of the beasts
heralding the dusk

I still don't know
what brings me here
what presses me to ride
off to these far flung points
to ferret out the corners
where secrets might be hid
somehow locked within the earth
for me to take and know

the drumbeat pulses
deep into the night
and is echoed by
the roll of thunder from afar
I touch inside a place
that knows all of these things
and builds of them enlightenment
forgotten in the dawn

- Brendan Tripp
07/29/1988

AUGUST 1988

8/2/88	HERE IN THIS WORLD
8/3/88	ANCIENT REASON AT THE LAST
8/4/88	TO DIE, EMBRACE THE NIGHT
8/5/88	THE GALLERY OF SIGHT
8/8/88	HAVING TICKETS FOR THE LIGHT
8/9/88	PERHAPS THE MANNER OR THE WAY
8/10/88	JUST ANOTHER NOXIOUS END
8/11/88	UNWHOLESOME WORLD, SO WORSE THAN DEATH
8/12/88	IN THE OPPRESSIVE WAITING
8/15/88	IN LAYERS OF THE VEIL
8/16/88	BOUGHT WITH THE BLOOD OF DREAMS
8/17/88	ANOTHER WRITING DOWN THE TUBES
8/18/88	IN THE UNDERTOW OF DAYLIGHT KEPT
8/19/88	HORIZONS OF PROCRASTINATION
8/22/88	NOT THE TIME OF VOICING PLEAS
8/23/88	AS DESIRE STILL SEEMS TO BE
8/24/88	PAUSING THE RUN OF LIFE
8/25/88	BASKETED IN STAVING
8/26/88	BATTLEMENTS TURNED TOWARDS THE DAY
8/29/88	PAUSING THROUGH THE WORD OF DAY
8/30/88	THE STORY OF THE MASSIVE DREAMS

HERE IN THIS WORLD

lateness brings the void
and empty is all I feel,
there is no purpose in day
and no hope within the night;
existence is a solitary road,
a pointless winding down of life
which tears insistent at the soul
leaving it bleeding, open,
prey to all emotions of despair
and memories of bittersweet might-have-beens
half seen through the tears of dire regret
shed against the swell of yesterdays lost

time conspires
to flood the mind
with visions
of stolen dreams

goodness leaks away from futures
and breath turns bitter in its age
making each tomorrow more filled with dread
and every thought more coiled in fear,
anticipating shocks hurled by the world
upon the flayed and open self;
a weight drops on the heart,
a lethargy enrobes the spirit
with cloaks with complications
on every action planned
and makes of time a wait for death,
a slow tick-tocking towards the grave

hopeless years
run through their turns
pointless rounds
on to decay

\- Brendan Tripp
08/02/1988

ANCIENT REASON AT THE LAST

times derive of shaking crystal
shudder, shatter
enveloping the course to take

    encircle now
    the tail and beak
    make whole the round
    and so return

we can not take the offered road
distant, dismal
into these discarded passings

    hold up to sky
    the blade of night
    transmute to grace
    the deity

the moment's pressing comes unstemmed
rushing, reeling
to force the hand dividing life

    swing censers round
    the altar's reach
    to focus will
    into the act

within regret solidifies
blocking, blasting
formed of scars on broken hearts

    crash into void
    the mind drops down
    emotion drowns
    in seas of dread

denied a recourse to clean ways
blissful, blessing
the broken soul reverts to pasts

    march to gallows
    strewn with flowers
    tis the season
    when all must die

- Brendan Tripp
08/03/1988

TO DIE, EMBRACE THE NIGHT

we are thrown into the pit,
this world of isolation;
damned, refused the mantle of the race,
buffeted by cruel despising
unfolded in rejection's venom
drenched with acid spite
    and anger here
    builds up its force
    and hatred here
    sears all our thoughts
    and madness here
    corrupts our being
    and living here
    becomes our death

my eyes stare wildly at the world
my teeth grit into bloody stumps
observing how these things deceive
in a universe so falsely made

        death
        becomes the focus
        center of this life
        darkness
        is the banner
        heralding that night
        rage
        becomes the power
        keeping us alive
        anguish
        is the poison
        stifling the light

the soul lies crippled
and prays to die
all strength is gone
to struggle at the chains
    there is a hatred of the self
    a loathing of that one within
the battle has been lost
no goodness walks these lands
we search for nightfall
and embrace the void
    there is no reason to exist
    in wastes so empty,
    days so blank

- Brendan Tripp
08/04/1988

THE GALLERY OF SIGHT

1
panes are removed
to let in unfiltered sight
harsh without
the bending of the rays

2
words flow in,
around, and through me;
I am lost in a sea
of churning expression

3
hope creeps into
the most unlikely breasts
sending up its flowers
to incredulous view

4
formed of night,
spawned in dark,
are there any that have known
the manner of this seed?

5
mobiles shift again,
wheels turn towards new alignment
and we detect a shift in names
almost desirous, almost devout

6
time comes diced
and then sautéed,
some burgoo mixing
of wild and nasty things

7
there are some breakings
sought within these fragile days;
a hammer waits within our kit
to schism pasts from running life

8
a thing of value
held jeweled in blue
rests awaiting
the ransom of the night

9
the tether lines pull tight
from all these many ways
each pulling, urging, yanking on
in opposition on our space

10
I know this manner
yet stay within the shadows
in indulgence of the whim
of the lilting cool and dark

11
from abysses now arise
the histories thought left behind
and, lo, the chalk is passed,
the voice must now be mine

12
there is no ease
on paths of grace
for power's price
is steep to pay

- Brendan Tripp
08/05/1988

HAVING TICKETS FOR THE LIGHT

in afternoon heat
and summer sun
as falling rays tinge
the walls with orange
the switch will flip
and power surge
and light will come
to Wrigley Field

home of ivy
home of day
blessed cradle
of the game
seventy three years
of sunlit ball
swing into history
this gleaming night

no longer sleeping
no longer still
burst with the vibrant
dark-piercing lamps
this old park boldly
comes of age
and trumpets futures
full of wins

yes, home of summer
afternoons, I will come
to see you shine
I will watch
your plays unfold
and cheer as loudly
for your Cubs
as in these many days

but how strangely
will come the end,
to file out into
some rowdy dark
and search the scoreboard
for the banner's tale
of "L" or "W" hung
out in that foreign night

- Brendan Tripp
08/08/1988

PERHAPS THE MANNER OR THE WAY

from there is brokered distance
not fair
     wheels spin out
     into chaos
     split from space
I know not from water
stripped as schism
spitting into steam
               night comes close
               is personal to the self
               erupts with flares unseen
the music is cut off
the edit is an axe
     not bartered into abeyance
     held more brutal than the still
     background light
but these
are not the ones observed
these become the stuff of time
reeled from greyness of the cells
in cellophane and colored tapes
          the memory holds little worth
          as files are scattered
          reality detained
     forthwith to arms
     forward to death
               for this, for this,
               the quote drops ashes
               and shrugs the bush
still, there are the little trails
which lead to places deep within
the pulsing madness of the whole
     hope leads, follows
     in trapdoors
     sprung again to empty falls
and all runs down
bled, discarded on the hook
pallid, vacant of the stare
                    it is here
                    that leaving starts
                    and newness opens
                    from the mire
no, nonetheless
these are disturbed
held down to counting
and misaligned

- Brendan Tripp
08/09/1988

JUST ANOTHER NOXIOUS END

1
sorest of sore subjects
comes up by night
by absence and isolation
unexpected, out of place
it burns a poker through the heart
and sprays acid on the soul
2
even by association
these faces sting
as memories assault the mind
peppering with the barbs of pain
as imaginings run wild
tearing through the gut
3
once more there is a love denied
once more the self has been defiled
thrown down to slime in torment
pressed face-first into shit
shown that the race has little use
for this being so despised
4
at every turn I see
fresh quanta of this hate,
every day confronts me
with new visions of despite
belittling the wounded core,
bleeding out the will to be
5
this world so full of lies
drives me forward onto death
there is no goodness
there is no truth
each word comes baited with the hooks
of agonizing pain
6
no comfort comes of company
when walls must be maintained
no solace stays in solitude
where loneliness awaits
all is bleakness, hateful, dark
an empty, killing ache

- Brendan Tripp
08/10/1988

UNWHOLESOME WORLD, SO WORSE THAN DEATH

somewhere inside
curled up
shaking through the spasms
of systems riding through
the agony of life...

    nothing is right
    the universe bleeds
    springs of decay

expenditures all outflow
from dollars to emotion
they fade to void
and build a gap within
there is no return
no inward flowing feed
this soul is dying
trapped in a vampire world
which saps the vital spark
and plunges my perceptions
into blackness
draped with death

    nothing is good
    and everything seeks
    to murder joy

the trap is sprung
and reality gives us no escape
all things have edges
sharp, cutting,
dimensions turn acute
to bring us pain
moisture beads on brows
and turns to acid
stripping off still sensate flesh
in sheets of seething gore
the air itself
thickens, gels
holds us in some amber gas
which poisons us for some display
in sadist sideshows
the form and being of this place
  this grinding center
  this unholy cavern
  this damned unceasing cage

- Brendan Tripp
08/11/1988

IN THE OPPRESSIVE WAITING

data runs backwards
years ago appear as now
there are themes that swirl
and resurface changed
their particulars shuffled
but in pattern still the same

we contemplate
exile into nature
and dictates made
so hard to be sustained

and so from nowhere
one of the pieces now appears

all our promises
have been destroyed
our vows to self
are shredded and burned
this place is growthless
made of stasis and stone

frustration
channels into rage
we are unhealthy
and sickness rots
the vortex points
there is no shining
the shell is locked
with bands of steel
and concrete
ten miles thick

hope and positivity
are smothered by the clouds
of storms that gathered
throughout the ages
to be thundering upon our life
apocalyptic and insane

there is no leaving
no exit but by death
there is no changing
no movement from this place
there is no staying
no weathering these gales

\- Brendan Tripp
08/12/1988

IN LAYERS OF THE VEIL

1
forthwith
there are three settled things
set in stone
in anger bled
turned from color
enraptured in the night

2
a segment's length
delineates our time
so divided
so taken from the then and here
that in confusion
flouncing comes
not given to defray the names
on other sides of calls

3
these are the blocks
poured from the box to floor
without a pattern
but that we see
without a reason
yet monkey hands they turn
and turn
and search the ways and whys
of these
in all their blankness

4
ensuing hours
break portals in the mix
insuring motion
matrix index of the dig
for the going
for absently made truth
that wants and needs and craves
the manner and the right

5
we are netted
pulled on board
in cold thin air
we awake
hard against the naked light
blinding, almost there

- Brendan Tripp
08/15/1988

BOUGHT WITH THE BLOOD OF DREAMS

no answer

anticipation rears
its crystal skull
fragile
in the bleeding light
burning
within the precincts
of the damned

all lost

we are dinosaurs
caught in shifting
levels of the real
there are plates
here on the move
there are layers
of embodiment
which grind against
each other's skin
          (while making one
          quite hellish din)

pulled down

all these doings
seem undone
the road of being
becomes unbearable
and empties into void
center
is uncherished
and cast away

bracketed

the pace has quickened
within some days
and presses at the chest
when tapped
pulse runs
as though the chase
was well set on
and hallowed sleep
was soon to break apart

- Brendan Tripp
08/16/1988

ANOTHER WRITING DOWN THE TUBES

use comes down
so small,
the hours break
in the crashing wake
of shattered power
and concepts lost

    to where?
    to where?

the words spill out
to blackness
and empty off the screen,
dimness wraps
itself around
the staring self
searching through the mind
for what has gone
now into dust

all this now
is gone
all this now
has slid

    to where?
    to where?

do those words
exist?
does that structure
still stand somewhere
in fleeting pasts
not held today
in this intrusive dark
denying all record,
remembrance and recall?

do perished poems
move on to life
in Akashic planes,
or simply drift
on morbid winds

    to where?
    to where?

- Brendan Tripp
08/17/1988

IN THE UNDERTOW OF DAYLIGHT KEPT

anticipation swells
through in surges
     overriding mind,
     overriding thought,
casting forms of dreams
within the mental space,
weaving webs of sweetness
of what may come to be

          I am shadowed
          by these clouds of doubt
          formed of hurts
          for years unhealed

          I am haunted
          by the thoughts of pain
          and failures
          for so long endured

once more it seems I journey
into these unset names
     seeking something,
     seeking blindly,
like lemmings driven
into the sea of death,
I set a course uncharted
and pray to be set free

          there is danger
          spoken of these ways
          hidden traps
          await my step

          there is peril
          in these darkened seas
          long distant
          and for long unseen

but then there comes the crash
and broken plans shatter
     transforming worlds,
     transforming self,
as change returns the slate
to blankness, new again,
strange and clear and open
to sow new seeds of hope

- Brendan Tripp
08/18/1988

HORIZONS OF PROCRASTINATION

time slips to nowhere
papers surface
dated more than years
ago
concepts form
and are delayed
pending runs to form a state
clips a spiral to a turn
in stasis to a cycle
waiting
goes to waiting
for the waiting
on through time

and
even seeing
does not break the lock
endless turning forms a field
halting motion
freezing hands
disallowing active modes
to snap apart the stable curve
of distanced moving,
deferred decisions,
put off purpose to beyonds
never quite within our grasp

minds
are machines
brains run circuits
on the blink
fuses blown
synaptic sparks
casting all to concrete grids
of what can go
and what can be
while
waiting
goes to waiting
for the waiting
on through time

- Brendan Tripp
08/19/1988

NOT THE TIME OF VOICING PLEAS

"It's 4:00,
do you know where
your Muse is?"

   - the unlikely
     and the not likely
   - the defrayed
     and the deferred

the construction of texts
                 of glyphs
                 of ancient
writings made anew
but annotated
to their form

     here comes the decision
     purchased from the other side
     here comes doubt
          arrayed in feathers
          multi-hued

the chopped-down days
run against the tide
aligning with obsession
given faces to their names

splash
     and action replays
protest
     forms the hold of ears
     in lamentation of the fall

          even in recall
          these colors move
               uninvolved,
               innocent,
          strictly in the way
          of outboard holdings
          of the truth

for these are hard,
they demand
     diagonals;
they have offered
my heart unto the sun

- Brendan Tripp
08/22/1988

AS DESIRE STILL SEEMS TO BE

1
the thought
the missing
it makes you crazy
it makes you itch
it brings a madness
to the running of the day
and locks the mind
into cycles of fixation
breaking down the focusing
fracturing one's being
     lower down
     all the power
     lower down
charge descends
through chakras
slipping from the head,
the heart,
pooling into basal drives
linked to primal needs
and overriding circuitry
of projects of the brain;
hardly thinking,
all a-churn

2
and there it is
almost
seeing is by force
all warped
     and mirages fill the mind
     where hope aligns the signals
     into semblance of need
and then the heart
is trapped
opened to the fates
and slashed

3
the world becomes a nightmare scene
lashed to chemicals and cravings
     and no needs are filled
     and no hopes are true
     and no prayers are answered
all degrades into murky dreams
full of pain and dread and anguish

- Brendan Tripp
08/23/1988

PAUSING THE RUN OF LIFE

artful incentive
necessity drive
making it restive
not nearly alive

broken down reasons
with no need to tell
turn of the season
descent into hell

schism allowance
permission to die
studied avoidance
with no where or why

purple and crimson
and drenched throughout sight
called upon jimson
allied with the night

told in the ashes
in ruins of halls
stars in their passes
and patterns of falls

words go to travel
as blades into time
space to unravel
in mystery crime

distant as ever
and deeper than fate
cords that we sever
return bearing hate

bastardized meaning
infused with desire
comes without gleaning
the truth of the fire

open resentment
and bald screaming rage
are the incitement
for shredding the page

quiet and stillness
descend on the tomb
in cyclic illness
accepting our doom

- Brendan Tripp
08/24/1988

BASKETED IN STAVING

becoming unseamed
this chokes
makes hazy
unfetters panic from its chain
flashing image runs the scale
in the thousands
disarrayed
all flies open, breaks apart
without explosion
unbided while
the habit courses into dark
here within
here alone
as assumption is unveiled
not quite real
amid regret
not handled well
as though there might be tape rewound
to do retakes
with later aspects grafted in
shuffled through the deck of cards
realigned
reassigned
brought to nothing in recall
splitting from the point of now
forgetting whether what we are
without the living
when and wither turns the past
into a beam
a focused light
that burns the brain
and sears the eyes
too sharp seeing in the haze
the murky depths of time slipped by
never held
lacking palpable delays
forever empty in return
hollowing the tactile gut
amassed unreally
arrayed unwell
fallen through the open door
to flow through channels undefined
unpredicted ways of length
forward with the blinding drive
of scoured runnings
and extended sighs

- Brendan Tripp
08/25/1988

BATTLEMENTS TURNED TOWARDS THE DAY

1
these hostilities
arise in concert
with the sickness
bled from burning lands

all open in light
all gone to seed

something's wrong with sight
and seeing fails to lead
faces have deserted names
and confusion churns the mind
against the rocks of hiding

all in goodness
all in time
the voice becomes
the word arrives

2
acts of existence
come shrouded, fogbound,
the perceptive points of need
are hinted far away

of these intrusions
little stays
they are brushings, pressures,
wisps in time

all empties down the abyss falls
cutting light in spectral bands
drowning out the ears by roar
all soaking, sodden,
stunned, maintained

because this here
is wasting
because this runs
to life

3
alas,
the night becomes
our palace tomb
against the hoards outside;
with wailing,
dirges, and despair,
we face the darkness
and open eyes to black

  it reaches to the outer wastes
  and cloaks the soul in grey

here dropped
here fallen
the reign has called
an ending

    throne room marble
    swept the dust
    in memorial
    decline

- Brendan Tripp
08/26/1988

PAUSING THROUGH THE WORD OF DAY

living in an
electroshock reality
where every turn
presents new pulses
writhing against
the essential mode of I
hammering away
at independent self
and trying to kill
the soul which dares
to stand apart

like that
you know
like that

And:
No matter where you go
and what you do there
will be people trying
their damnedest to make
you conform to some
concept they have about
how everything, including
you, should ought to be
and ought to do; the real
grind comes when you find
that they do not represent
a coherent conformity,
instead they all feel that
they and they alone are
the one true arbiter of
The Norm and assume that
everybody else is simply
trying to irritate them.

I say:
Kill 'em all.
Nuke the bastards
'till they glow.

day all chains
huddles down in grief
pouring mass on tearing heart
unable to withstand the glare
of novas blasting bright with rage

- Brendan Tripp
08/29/1988

THE STORY OF THE MASSIVE DREAMS

1
there is:

  a dropping, sinking
  feeling of despair

  a sense of foreboding
  laced with dread

  an insulating veil
  which blinds us from sight

  a panic that grips
  with nails of iron

and perception shifts
from one to the other
on through the waking

2
there are random searching
play modes in operation
shifting tunes within the brain
  they theme the day
  and slave the word
  into their sway
in grasp they run to garble
in recall they decline

3
and here we have
another curse
meted out
from those on high
  inception of the action
  direction of the wait
it is the going
the form to be
allowed
the slicing of the time
    segmented
    perceived
here in the window form
of life
taken with breezes
held aloft to die
      perhaps to dream
or is this solely itself
the dream
broken into beings?

4
long distance awaiting
bide the moment of instruction
     the answer of inquiry
     the lining of interpretation
for the telling
to the world
          it comes with tendrils
          born of blame
          bled from passage
and is then greeted
with new blankness
     much like death
     with ash for eyes

5
I seek a cleansing
to wash my hands
of these modes of life
to rinse away
the foulness of existence
     so bound to dust
     so mired in slime
I would step away,
move back from here,
pull the core
off from this place,
reenter corners
much like sleep
which harbor strange
new forms of seeing
     away from heartache
     away from pain
I so yearn
to crack the chain
which binds me to
this living

6
and there they are
aligned with reason
reality's new issued lies
     here comes knowing
     here comes belief
where all are blindness
and sleep the sleep
locked into the tale
          await the axeman
          await the blade
and know the edit comes too late

- Brendan Tripp
08/30/1988

SEPTEMBER 1988

9/1/88	UNSUSPECTED PANIC HERE
9/2/88	POINTS TO PLACEMENT FORMING
9/6/88	A SICKNESS, DEATH TO TIME
9/7/88	WITHIN THE AFTER, PAST THE NOON
9/8/88	AND SPEAKING NOT THE SEEN
9/9/88	STRANGE WITHIN THE CONTACT SPACE
9/10/88	WRONG AFTERNOON ENCHAINED
9/13/88	TO BE SO DAMNED AGAIN
9/14/88	THE DEATHLY MODES OF HATE
9/15/88	IN BLASTED NIGHT ALONE
9/16/88	FAR TOO BUSY TO MOVE OR THINK
9/17/88	IN CHURNING TIME APPROACHING GONE
9/22/88	IMAGE PARTING, SO LONG HELD
9/23/88	AMID THE MOTION CLAD OF TIME
9/24/88	THE UNEXPECTED COME AGAIN
9/25/88	WITHIN THE DARK, THE MOTION, SPACE
9/26/88	BAD PLACE WORSE WITHIN
9/27/88	THE PLACE IS NOT THE PAIN
9/28/88	DIRECTIONS AMID THE DAY
9/29/88	TRIPARTITION OF ALL THINGS SAID
9/30/88	BATHED IN FOULEST LIFE

UNSUSPECTED PANIC HERE

clashing of insurgence
     what is here
     is scheduled there
     what from there
     now settles here
there are no times for resting
for ease of habit, ease of pace
all is hurtling on
unasking our assent
not caring why we tarry

     unwilling I structure
     months into these days
     with jettisoned concept
     and stress against the well

the mind
has not
prepared itself
the frame
has not
been stretched to fit
the self
has not
a scheme for this
the time
has not
followed its course

     without the forming mold
     these things move unchecked
     there is no unused space
     no safety net for me

panic is the object
     not enough,
     the hours fall
     lists run through
     the sleepless night
who crafts these frantic beings
agendas of the brutal press
built of our distance
shaken in surprise
and open to dismissal?

- Brendan Tripp
09/01/1988

POINTS TO PLACEMENT FORMING

1
we are asked of these distances
and are dumbfounded
blank with naught to say
2
rage smears from darkness and neglect
swords flash mighty
as they stab and stab again
3
before the dissolution comes
there is a reminiscence
of new place and pointlessness
4
we stand here empty
as with a broken toy
and know not how the all was lost
5
all good things become the victim
of the sorrow and despite
that warp the universe's turns
6
at times belief is not withheld
and traps form from the air
but not again, no not again
7
the tones of flesh and curves of form
blast echoes through the mind
yet falling through the years they fade
8
have stars spoken on the page
and charted out the form of night
into these unknown lands?
9
time bleeds sickly into dust
and hands us things of stone
all but to go, all but to go
10
there is denouncement's path
sharp and hard to take while sane
yet boiling to the blood
11
because of thee they all lack voice
and nameless they become
for these are halls of thine alone
12
and so is done the seeding
as dictates are obeyed
reality bows down to will

- Brendan Tripp
09/02/1988

A SICKNESS, DEATH TO TIME

a blasted feeling
deep inside
tearing through
the shattered gut
     floating somehow
     outside,
     beyond

here idles uselessness
here the waves
of anguish threaten
to wash over the barriers
and drown us in their bile
     I am so lost
     so empty
     so denied

there is no goal to striving
each day is cloaked
in fog decreed
to simple running out
shattered from purpose
wasted in decay
     who are these people
     why do they move
     why be?

each option falls
somehow unneeded
goodness bleeds from self and world
not taking shape
just leaving, gone
     here is void
     here is death
     taken like a pill

I am that poison
within the soul
I breathe that aching
and wish to die
     disappointment
     gathers round,
     awaiting

- Brendan Tripp
09/06/1988

WITHIN THE AFTER, PAST THE NOON

sense pulses through
the hours of existence

imaginings form
impressions linger
emotions surge like tides amok
     berserk without regard
     to reason's tender

frames shift in
and out
changing like the gels
on spotlights
illuminating worlds
in biased hues
tinting perception
to the colors of their sway

          what is long
          comes short
          what is short
          runs into eternities

known/unknown
musics unfold
     within the head,
     how grey stuff plays
     the lead and rhythm?

the various assorted needs
and insistent things apply
for options
on our time
they allow no space for breath
no cool retreat's redemption

          absolutes
          are not attained
          all is bargained
          arbitrated

better modes deny
towards the pressing day
set down
confused
complete

- Brendan Tripp
09/07/1988

AND SPEAKING NOT THE SEEN

you are encircled
taken in by force outside
you have enabled
the makings of this siege
and
pause
and all falls backwards
spilling into realms of dreams
touched as a wall
when lost in reading
read as details
in trapped sand
and
now enfold
pulling around the world as cloak
changing relationships
angles bend and warp the lines
curving into piercing points
swirling vision into self
rushing madly faster where
eternity upon itself
within itself
amid the self
apart
isolated
bridged but lightly
to the "real"
blind, unknowing
what that was
what agreements held that state
and
so return
surface lightly from the depths
float through darkness ever up
pressing onward to the waves
awaiting at the shore
to crash
to shatter stillness
to churn without within
blasting storm-tossed at the rocks
unsuspected far below
here in naked light displayed
alienated from the calm
and
is this real
is this so bright and empty?

- Brendan Tripp
09/08/1988

STRANGE WITHIN THE CONTACT SPACE

bang bang
     who are these people
     jumping out of the past?
these files are closed
written off
they have no business
no need
          I swim confused in this
          I do not have coordinates
          to point me in this way

chop chop
losses cut
now spring back as a debt
     but not my owing
     nor my wish to take
this collection
requires reordering
of far too many mental sets
          I balk at motion
          I doubt the form
          and know not how to act

never never
did I think
that there would be return
     of this
     of these
yet now in difference
now there has been change
and lacks the promise
which was so strong before
          I find this tempting
          I yet desire
          but still retreat the solo way

alas alack
all this comes back
it is decisive
in its indecision,
clearly seen,
inscrutable
     the pages fall empty
     the lines are left unsaid
self seems unworthy in this place
held hostage by its hopes and dreams
          I am unnamed among the names
          I am unknowing among the known
          and empty in the full of life

- Brendan Tripp
09/09/1988

WRONG AFTERNOON ENCHAINED

1
perfect days
arise so seldom
     clad in temperatures
     that go unnoticed
     stirred by breeze
     that is not wind
somehow these
are always scuttled
by schedules
that care not for the day
and will not bend
to take the pleasures
of easy times
outside

2
words run to
completion
their repetition
ceases and lies still
     a heavy breath escapes
     that doneness has arrived
the tasks of ages
seem to stretch
forever across the year
with no end
no reprieve
a wall comes rushing up in time
and threatens its increase
lest the cycle start again

3
these are the actions
manifesting of our chain
     from other sides
     these dictates issue
     that work be done
     beyond the compass of the mind
and so the hours tick away
in silence, solitude,
isolation and intent;
in this is a building,
a blind amassing
of unknown design,
here harbors but the hoping
that these are modes of growth

- Brendan Tripp
09/10/1988

TO BE SO DAMNED AGAIN

it feels so bad
as suicide's veil
drops across my eyes
and darkens living
into some ashen play

     no hope or plans stand
     within this space;
     the only real futures
     are ones bearing death

I can not understand
how life becomes so bad,
how little rejections
can build to years of bitter solitude
crushing by the very weight
of empty time

     there are no good things,
     only poisons enwrapped
     in cynical pretense,
     false joys hiding pain

each time
the heart is opened
it is abused,
torn to shreds
and mocked in its despair

     I have no strength
     to walk among the race,
     their day is darkness
     smothering my soul

what use is there in being
when I am plainly damned?
how could any seething hell
torment the self more than this world
which thirsts for my destruction,
delights in my decay?

     I seek the form of leaving,
     the weapon of demise;
     I would will this absence
     to break me clean away

- Brendan Tripp
09/13/1988

THE DEATHLY MODES OF HATE

1
all these tremors hit
as mood swings wildly
shaking the structure
and the course of day
     depression
     now enters
     opens eyes
     to shadows
there are no patterns
by which to gauge the
coming of these pains
no way to avoid death
2
and so,
again comes the twisting
again comes the torment
built of blindness
faced with stone
fueled by hatred
of all that I am
     I would die
     I will die
     I rather die
     than to live within your world
here is the blade,
here the flesh,
let all flow crimson
on the shoddy pieces,
detritus of your will
3
all within has burned to vacuum
the self that meets the world
has devolved to nothing
your hand has made me all ashes and void
I am hollow, charred, and acid-bled,
crushed and crumbled, ground into vileness,
these are what you make me now
          finish this,
          take now this life
          away that you have ruined
          wasted in its biding cell
          kill me blindly
          as you destroy yourself
          unknowing give me
          my revenge

- Brendan Tripp
09/14/1988

IN BLASTED NIGHT ALONE

1
too few things are pending
within this life,
too few nouns combine
to form its texture
     its verbs
     run in one vein
there is small spectrum
of how we can exist
or how we do
when slid between
the grim and sad
lashed on depression's grid
2
within the night
as in all nights
there is an anguish
clutched upon the heart
     its seed is loneliness
     and years without a mate
this washes sorrow
in waves across the mind
and makes the thoughts of death
take hold
3
again
the brain will scramble
to scatter plans
with no hope to complete,
and clutch at straws
that speak of future goodness
that stands apart
from all that's known today
     the feedback loop
     will not accept
     defeat, denial,
     it turns again
     the course of life
     into the teeth of pain
4
and years go on
with age not building worth
     more loss than gain
     comes to the self
as false delusions strip away,
the naive hopes lost to the light
of ugly being,
unpleasant life,
leaving just the crippled core,
naked, shredded in the wind

- Brendan Tripp
09/15/1988

FAR TO BUSY TO MOVE OR THINK

too much opens
within one day's bounds
as fatigue hits
and drains the form of strength

    within this comes
    departure
    amid these preparations
    gels an end

all goes blank
runs neutral
takes apart the will and wants
in litter of that state

    the seeing stares
    off at the sun
    and all is waiting
    primed for sleep

priorities
shift and change
as lists still scream
from dark of mind

    there are the must-do's
    the need-to-be's
    they crowd and badger
    dragging down the ghost

searching comes within us
scanning takes the helm
and shuffles through the chaos
for how the night shall be

    because's run
    ahead of buts
    justifying
    no relief

- Brendan Tripp
09/16/1988

IN CHURNING TIME APPROACHING GONE

1
chart these places
align these times
form of line and number
the matrix of a life
spent running from center
playing tag with the leper self
     these
     are the ways the flow is cut
     this
     breaks apart continuity
     and shatters vales of dreams

2
prepare for absence
many ways
not in the mode
of habitual displacement
     yet there are cycles
     seen upon the page
     pulses returning
     again and again

3
and here there is the self
cut down, debased,
thrown into this exile
by each successive queen
     the executioner's axe
     is almost wished
     to make and end
     to all this grieving

4
almost as though machines ran time
and cogs and gears pulled through the days
in being-mills whose packaging
bore brands with Tuesday, Wednesday names
whose expiration dates arrive
as soon as they move off the line
     the schedule
     is the truer way
     there is scant life
     within these lines
     run through the calendar's decay

- Brendan Tripp
09/17/1988

IMAGE PARTING, SO LONG HELD

missing visage
     lost to time
     and forgetting
almost like sand
run through hands
made long with hours
of dull extension

     we miss this
     yes
     it breaks the flow
     makes gaps
     hollows out the history
          and saddens
          in future sense of loss

changes now
become less clear
     they are moving
     within the dark
the numbered run
of days and dates
has caught us up
     has broken with
     the light

          and meanwhile
          there turn new concerns
               of placement
               pointing and
               decision
          the span is wracked
          by doubt and fear
          unholy by the falling page

still digits drop
in absent sight
     a pile amasses
     built of passage
not holding to the dream
we are abrupt
and nullified
spread to tantamount ideals
which dry and wither
     and move like dust
     off on the wind

- Brendan Tripp
09/22/1988

AMID THE MOTION CLAD OF TIME

1
pausing in the rush
obliterating schedules
opening the time to breathe
and hope that nothing happens
    like the world stops
    or we lose our place
    or that the dream deflates
    into ashes and the grayest void
2
panic is the theme
of this segment,
stress is the winding
driving on this life
        3
        there are
        no reasons
        no places
        no truths
4
and yet,
something good seems to come,
from threats of anguish
bursts this promise
      clad in doubt
      but split apart
      from dread that went
      before
5
excitement pulses through the wait
of long time musics brought to stage
combined at last in ancient haunts
accessed in presence, brief and hard
          6
          if but to dream
          of better ways
          for future forms
          to gel tonight
    7
    also is the hope,
    the prayer,
    to pull these riches
    deep within
      arrayed in silver,
      in flesh and sweet,
      built of reason
      pure and perfect

- Brendan Tripp
09/23/1988

THE UNEXPECTED COME AGAIN

sad day
sorry day
broken day
thrust into time
     stripped of reason,
     eclipsed from plan,
     into vagueness
     sent denied all dreams

where is the backing,
where the group
that would fit
around the self?
     all is solitude,
     the feeling spark within the void
     without true contact
     not greeted or well hailed

there seems no point
to justify continuing,
the soul lies wasted
among the ruins of this life
     there is an ache
     that runs deeper than the bone,
     an emptiness
     that stretches beyond time

why am I amid this world,
where do I belong,
who is this I
that anguish so attends?
     no purpose seems to come;
     all doings fall to dust,
     my striving crumbles
     and hopes are bitter lies

the years turn surely on
and age creeps to the form
there is but grey before me
and blackness close behind
     a pall is cast on breath
     and death stares from my eyes,
     the course of being
     has drained to pools of ash

- Brendan Tripp
09/24/1988

WITHIN THE DARK, THE MOTION, SPACE

1
strange presence
undrowned
by light of full moon,
are you neighbor world
made visible
by this your close return?
you stand undimmed,
unmoving,
yet harbor not the red
which my suspicions
would detect

2
on top of clouds
are shadows
cast by passing planes,
this, our plane
on which we fly,
strange shadow there
with rainbow aura
rung around
as if to prove
the contrariness of light
in both its forms revealed

3
unsettled space
with hours juggled,
stripped of sleep
yet rushing headlong to that state
none of these things
are we to do
but count the backlog of the night
in lengthy stretches to the day
made one with seeing
wrapped into sight
occluded from the absent dream

- Brendan Tripp
09/25/1988

BAD PLACE WORSE WITHIN

what comes purchased
in this time?
what is stolen
from this life?

    these days are too much filled
    with stress and dreading,
    recalcitrance and fear,
    they live too much
    within the shallows of division,
    torn apart
    from native inner ways

the hours fall unwell
all sickness hits the mind
each segment alters
to be aligned with untoward states
mad, incarnate
of everything that is against
what harbors here the good

    pain then enters
    as the theme
    and agony
    as the truth

        I seek the chance to leave
        to slip away unnoticed
        while shedding bonds
        off to some hazy side
        and fade all channels
        into other
        less structured modes

this is full wrong
for me and for my kind
I stand at distances
and am dumbfounded
all agape at what I see
in worlds of action
insane places of churning need

    dictate reason
    of the time
    despair ever
    whole to be

- Brendan Tripp
09/26/1988

THE PLACE IS NOT THE PAIN

far is this going
unsteady the air
long runs the time
hard upon the mind
     disturbance comes
     and makes me think of death
and death,
this hangs close
to thinking's flow,
within return there is such doubt
that familiar places
bring familiar pain
and that there never
will be new love,
never a release
from the isolation of these years
     there seems no use,
     no promise in these days
still, days turn
on into further days,
there is no stopping,
there is no change,
heading onward without goal
pointless in the living act
so much like death,
so empty, grey, and vile
     no good is here,
     inside has nothing reached
so just location
shifts in time,
just the place
which sites our pain,
cursed, we bear the massive shell
of walls denying any breach
that could bring joy
into this world
or sweetness into
bitter life
     alas, no hope
     can penetrate this heart
a blackness surrounds
the flighted inside
like dark within
a murdered soul

- Brendan Tripp
09/27/1988

DIRECTIONS AMID THE DAY

1
the inner elements of rage
allow nothing to be done
spurred by screaming
bent by barbs
all systems tighten to a knot
and balk at movement
halt the action
cold and dead

2
unheralded come these words
too late, it seems, too late;
divorced from meaning,
sent to all who care,
they tumble to the world
confused and blinded
denied their history
     what ritual
     must shape these
     that they may hold
     the key?

3
attention falters
into the weary state
too many things are musts
and all things seem so strange
again our time distends
and we are left without a gauge
to filter through these feelings
and find an end to day

4
nothing here
there is nothing
I reach inside
and find vacuum
where should be soul
I look outside
and see but void
     no colors are found
     but ashen grey
     no living is found
     but walking death

- Brendan Tripp
09/28/1988

TRIPARTITION OF ALL THINGS SAID

1
dropped into
truncated insistence
squeezed down to shortness
spewing list right after list
mechanical shifting
prioritizing on the fly
hoping all slots into place
when returning comes to call
    hey,
    these are plans
    we did not plan for
    additions made
    without informed consent

2
irritants arrive
borne on pages
borne on lines
they sneak uneases into mind
which churns them into froth
thick and sticky
which gums up all the normal works
with thoughts of unknown need
    uh-oh,
    bad plans are coming
    of digging deeper
    into dusty wells
    now much like graves

3
schemes grow crystal
across the softness of the brain
to overload intending
and make a situation freeze
to definition
sliced and diced and made to say
which manner of a thing it is
in doubtless modes of pain
    damn,
    even when we see it coming
    we still lead with the chin
    oh, foolish death-wish,
    oh, stupid ass

- Brendan Tripp
09/29/1988

BATHED IN FOULEST LIFE

1
blasted is the alteration
void and static
it is heavy
          a mass
          amassed
made untrue
in scathing light
     seared by glare
     not of the time

2
somewhere within
is reaching,
pressing on frustration's walls,
emitting discomfort,
exuding the bile
of misapportioned worlds
     this is the wrong
     pretending
     to be right

3
and, if a dream
why not a wake?
          awoke
          to deeper sleep
there are no bodies in the haze
no form to concept
amorphous yet immanent
     hard set to panic
     abutting on the face

4
here now I see,
to me comes vision
and turns the gut
     are not these true
     for sake of illness?
it breaks back into going
the lines of placement
          of gone/
          not gone

5
life bleeds out
everything becomes too short
divided from intent
     there arises dying
     from poisoned seed
     hidden in the soul
no continuity
weaves in this time
all is rough, particulate

6
and there are reasons
enmeshed in flowing tears
rhymes of purpose
transgressing laws of space
     but blindness
     is on the heart
     darkening the earth
sad falls knowing
sadder still belief

- Brendan Tripp
09/30/1988

OCTOBER 1988

10/3/88 DRAINING TOWARDS THE BLACK
10/4/88 AS LOWER PLACES, THESE
10/5/88 THAT SUICIDE MAKE FREE FROM HELL
10/6/88 DASHED AND HAZY, SO PERPLEXED
10/7/88 WRONGLY FOUND AMID RIGHT TIME
10/10/88 THIS FORMED FROM ACHING DARK
10/11/88 SWEPT UP WITHIN THAT RUSHING TIDE
10/12/88 POLARITY'S REPULSION, PAIN
10/13/88 AS PLACED WITHIN THE CHRONIC STREAM
10/14/88 THE WAY TO FORMING SIGHT
10/15/88 APART, ALONE, AWAITING
10/16/88 IN WASTED STATES FORLORN
10/17/88 OUT THROUGH THOSE REALMS OF SIGHT
10/18/88 ALWAYS, ALWAYS, ALWAYS RAGE
10/19/88 A GOODNESS NEVER QUITE ATTAINED
10/20/88 SOMETIME SOME WAYS
10/21/88 THE FROZEN FLOW OF DEATH
10/24/88 PART OF THESE DECAYS
10/25/88 FORMING PER THE LIGHT DESIGNED
10/26/88 FINAL SANDS WE TENSE AWAIT
10/29/88 WOODED, DISTANT, NOT QUITE RIGHT

DRAINING TOWARDS THE BLACK

uh-oh
here is
bottom
again
    (much like
     death,
     much like
     dying)
and like
dying
it has
its pains,
and like
death
it bears
darkness
    (no, no,
     all appears
     negative,
     blackness
     takes the place
     of light)
alone,
cut off,
divided
from love,
exiled
from care
    (solitude
     is the cell,
     loneliness
     forms the chain)
I am sick,
the body
will not bear
this curse
    (systems
     fade out,
     failing,
     corrupt)
and here
is empty,
self is
uncaring
for life,
existence

- Brendan Tripp
10/03/1988

AS LOWER PLACES, THESE

so hard,
difficulties cloud
the mind,
make slow and stupid
all attempts

          and depression
          drags us down

there seem new threads
of uselessness
within the fabric of the world
     as if
     vague options
     have now died
this sending takes
fresh meaning then
          forming the clarion
          sounding the dirge

     tides are tearing
     at our mass
     pulling open
     the inner void

still new spins
are made,
dame Fortune
must be wooed again
          and combinations
          strike strange in day
          patterns
          not run before
but without hope,
resigned to trying's chain

               outside are eyes
               unimpassioned
               unimpressed

and yet,
these are inner clouds,
the heart
is torn and tarnished
and all down

- Brendan Tripp
10/04/1988

THAT SUICIDE MAKE FREE FROM HELL

frustration throttles
all my insides
it clutches up
on my breath, my muscles
tense and try to twist
the life out of the form
struggling against
a killing world,
a hell,
a place of dying made insane
by faulty action,
faulty dream

    It is impossible
    to work,
    all tools now speak of death.
        My blades,
        these turn towards my shaking wrists.
        My pencils, pens,
        these long to be thrust through my gut.
        And, my machines,
        these tempt me with their power surge,
        to walk through water with their kind
        turned on, to crackle, hiss, and die.

damning, damned,
and damnable world,
pit of torment,
keep of pain,
how greatly I desire your death
or lacking that the death of me
that I be free
of your cruel treasons,
be released
from endless cycles of denial,
endless anguished rounds of hate,
crushing repetitions built
of hopes destroyed
and prayers melted in cold light
sung in wailing screams
which echo your corrupt desires
    where only evil is for real
    and only agony can be felt
    and only dying can make free
    within this grey
    and ashen place

- Brendan Tripp
10/05/1988

DASHED AND HAZY, SO PERPLEXED

1
depression,
thine name;
wailing insanity,
thine mark
     2
     urges thus:
          to kill,
          destroy;
          make empty,
          make void
3
and are these
shaped of vision?
     4
     power,
     rage,
     frustration,
     anger!
5
and in slight moments a clearness comes,
washed with places and people past,
where light beyond the eyes had entered
and touched with joy a place inside
     6
     where,
     this goes
     to where?
7
there is brutality
set in breath,
there are unsettlings
amid the day,
     there comes unreason
     and thoughts of death,
     there seem no freeing,
     no saving way
8
are not there better,
can this be all there is?
          9
          and allow
          new growth
          to come
          to being
10
I am uncertain in these days
unstable and unsure of life

- Brendan Tripp
10/06/1988

WRONGLY FOUND AMID RIGHT TIME

news breaks into
places of residal
and sometimes gladdens
     how come response
     becomes so hard?
these are tidings welcome, known,
and yet some distance creeps in here
and ices up the flow of words
far from the page

     now is season
     of the wind,
     leaving is pressed
     on gusts of cold
     into spaces
     crisp and free

but freedom never comes within,
never touches at the soul
     mind races to find
     locales of no chain
     but falls empty
          stupid in
          a limit sphere
are we destined
forever to this way,
to see these states in vision
but to always live denied?
     so clear
     sometimes
     so wholly seen
     but never felt
          never granted us
          inside

     old turns come
     again renewed,
     stupid in return;
     these bear hope
     upon the heart,
     foreboding to the mind

this is the breaking of the fall,
the hollowness that eats the soul
when all is dying but the self
and placement lies so wrongly set

- Brendan Tripp
10/07/1988

THIS FORMED FROM ACHING DARK

there we go
among the dead
amid the dark
sudden breaking culls a place
to form intent and goal
in northward journeys set
     grope through
     nights of chill
     in darkness
          set the coil,
          define intent,
     make circles
     for the long time stay

          edges somehow soften
          in attitude in this
          jarring situations smooth
          and leave only an ache
          residual from the rage

so, now we go
for waiting,
as for release,
things split open in these nights
and place insistence counter sleep
to make these calls
     is number
     key to this,
     have days been set
          to open,
          to alter routes,
     are these names
     touched by silent screams?

not against this,
not allowed;
     the vision runs spotty,
     too misty to be grabbed
     and unable to detail
we thus await the trial
which comes of ice and time
and weakness and desire
held to sacred ground
     for fear of moving
     for fear of loss
     for fear of absent things retained
          in forms unknowing
          in shadows of the mind
     and what has come to be
     no more

where we go
we go alone
where our seeing
leads our searchings into
is a land uncharted
spoken of in whispers
     fly now
     in seeing
     attain this
          in swiftness
          in sure intent
     take the day
     beyond the present

          no doubt must be allowed
          nor weakness let enter
          to the keep of our resolve
          for here are germs of change
          all glittering with power

- Brendan Tripp
10/10/1988

SWEPT UP WITHIN THAT RUSHING TIDE

"I would find the places
 where they sleep more lightly,
 as I sleep more lightly;
 I would awake, oh, God, I would awake!"

these spirits
come again,
their visitations
hit hard within my life;
they are as
an unknown star
whose tidal pull
tears all my will away
in the violence of its wake
 and I am bled out,
 naked to the other side,
 angry and unsure,
 unable to see,
 unable to know,
 blinded and beset by winds,
 adrift on turgid seas

 if such is brought
 by preparation,
 how much more
 shall enter in the act?

there is a flow
in this ride,
I feel a pattern
leading on
 as days fall into the abyss,
 emptying on cataracts of time
there shall be journals kept there,
I feel explosions of the word
now pending to be born,
awaiting in the wings
for hours of discomfort,
for cold distressing time
 the tribe is pulled around,
 the lineage retained
in this might come
the focus of release
in the season of return
at locations of desire,
in this might come
the strengthening
against that day-lit night

- Brendan Tripp
10/11/1988

POLARITY'S REPULSION, PAIN

still alone,
still without,
all things fail,
all attempts
to break out from this cage
are failures,
are shot down in ashes,
denied to even flame
briefly, brightly,
they drop stillborn,
as dead as hopes or dreams
butchered by a freezing world
which locks me here
deep within,
isolated and apart

every victory
comes as defeat,
every growth
within the self
is poisoned,
plundered,
seen as dying
and decay,
here without context
in the world,
here without contact
in the heart

agonies build up
in days and months and years
forming histories,
sad tales of living
not quite lived,
and being
not quite become

in this the self is framed,
is set like faulty jewels
in a useless, worthless piece;
no running moves away
from the center of corruption,
the imperfection here
which flays the soul
and creates a loathing
in all who come too near

- Brendan Tripp
10/12/1988

AS PLACED WITHIN THE CHRONIC STREAM

1
much too bad
much too many
falling down
knocked into
realms of falsehood
     dominos
     tiles of days
     tumbled
     ill wind blows
     all good down
2
expectation crumbles
badness curdles
into worse
vile and foul
unsettled
     here comes doubt
     and paranoia
     here is wishing
     to be gone
     to be away
3
tick and tick
the clock runs on
to calendar turf
making momentum
all uncontrolled
     not ready
     not prepared
     claws reach for time
     fall empty
     with only air
4
split from reason
sheared off from worlds
of long inurement
pierced by ice
and duration's lead
     tear now
     from eyes that see
     all the fears
     of what will come
     and what must be

- Brendan Tripp
10/13/1988

THE WAY TO FORMING SIGHT

1
altered visuals
perspective shifts
in this going
in this hour
the physical mode
is realigning
in the hunger
and the wait
2
memories flash
of bus rides made before
of images set
in flashing perception
stored up in words
for time not quite attained
within unsteadiness,
hope and doubt and fear
3
the sun has almost set,
the moon, a sliver,
gives scanty light
with which to make the heavens lined
and the directions known;
how is the power then to come
drawn down to points
of unsure placement?
4
discomfort comes with company
amid these journey's miles
mind runs towards focus
to pointing and a goal
so ill defined
a hazy end well hid
by drapings of the form
and the discipline to sit
5
the road, then,
points the way,
no other guidance
is harbored here;
our action
is the search,
our searching
is the deed

- Brendan Tripp
10/14/1988

APART, ALONE, AWAITING

isolation
in forests,
on bluffs
overlooking water,
amid the turning trees;
here is circle,
here duration,
a world apart
alone with me
     there are creatures here,
     creatures that awake
     with rustles, scratching,
     noise against the filtered sounds
     of cars, trains, boats and planes

awaiting runs
to halfway,
weakness
attaches to the form,
sleep comes drifting strangely
both in and out,
all seems hazy
yet somehow clear
within intent
     sun now sets with warmth
     yet I dread the cold
     that shook me freezing
     cruelly into waking states
     and shuddered my resolve

I now prepare
for long night,
for cold
to come again and test
the mettle of my soul
in nature set,
in leaf surround,
amid this long
waiting to see
     these hungers nibble
     and press insistent
     for food or vision
     amid the lonely question
     within the falling dark

- Brendan Tripp
10/15/1988

IN WASTED STATES FORLORN

another place
of emptiness
where reaching inwards
garners void,
another place
without a change,
just same imprisoned,
suicidal me
     what good is there
     in going out
     to isolated spots
     to sit and fast
     and seek to see
     some vision of true self
     when there are only
     glimpses made,
     tempting morsels
     of some other life
     beyond these walls,
     beyond that darkened glass
it always feels
that death must come
to make me finally free
from all these weights
and all these lies
which twist existence
into worlds of hell
and make me not quite me
     what good is searching
     within this cell,
     amid this stone and chain?
     all I can see
     of truer worlds
     are cruel glimmers,
     hints and echoes,
     and none to bring the key
     to break me from
     this dungeon here
     and let me be away
inaction brings
no good at all
yet striving does the same
all wasted, null,
thrown to the void,
it falls to ashes
and pleads for grace
that's never to be seen

- Brendan Tripp
10/16/1988

OUT THROUGH THOSE REALMS OF SIGHT

for this is the manner
in which the past is retrieved
     pulled from nightmares
     simmering in the juices
     of a psyche gone awry
lines erupt
and go faulty
eyes stare wildly
at distances not attained
thoughts careen
from infinity to the grave
and hold a vigil
sweaty in the palm of time
     this is the entrance
     the vale of knives
     through these doorways
     have passed all those who see
no ground supports me
no haven shields my mind
I am all pulse
an organism wildly paced
run ragged, naked, and insane,
beholden only to that drive
insistent, forward, on and on
     steel congeals to challenge stone
     all is cutting, acid, sharp,
     the form inverts, in to out,
     cadaver gruesome yet alive
here there is folding
here dimensions cease and bend
senses shift to other modes
and every vector realigns
     cardinals, where are you now,
     familiar spirits lose their shape
     directions shatter in vortex drag
over here
over there
sense still mingles
amid the chaos, madness, whirl
there is a center
somehow a self
within this forms a point of mind
which reaches out to grasp the world
and in its reach
encompasses the whole
     no lines now
     no demarcations
     there is no other apart from self
     no holding, held,
     no seer, seen

against the churning
memory attains
scatter-shot reason
whole histories detailed
spun into lineages beyond time
repeated, redoubled,
branched in layers in nameless states
which curl and curl
back on themselves
becoming altered, becoming changed
yet standing into unique space
unlabeled, undefined
     each universe is born herein
     no meaning bides in time
     eternal, momentary
     clicking through durationless
and this, and here
the mists relieve
again the form clears out
to old, familiar,
and mundane worlds
not shifted in their lines
     so, too, the problem,
     perhaps the curse
     that from the outer bounds returns
     to one again
     always the first

- Brendan Tripp
10/17/1988

ALWAYS, ALWAYS, ALWAYS RAGE

bash, smash, crash,
crush, devour, destroy

    all twisted
    all twisted up
    tension grinds
    within, inside
        I want to kill
        I want to maim
        all I touch
        becomes at risk
        all I see
        pull tighter bands
        upon my soul

bash, smash, crash,
crush, devour, destroy

    demon things
    demon things burn
    rage inside
    with fiery hate
        I am distressed
        I am destroyed
        all of me
        is loathsome flame
        all I am
        is fraying brain
        and tattered nerves

bash, smash, crash,
crush, devour, destroy

    no saving
    no saving grace
    here for me
    no path to calm
        I feel the hate
        I feel the rage
        all the world
        seeks death for me
        all my heart
        desires to die
        or make them die

bash, smash, crash,
crush, devour, destroy

- Brendan Tripp
10/18/1988

A GOODNESS NEVER QUITE ATTAINED

morning clutters up the mind,
chopping at the neater sleep
with questions of alarms and day,
from sweet oblivion roughly drags
into unwelcome light
     and
     there she was
     one line away,
     just one dimension shift
     apart
how close an absence
this can be
when all but there
I sense she was
holding, loving,
soft and warm
throbbing in some morning sweetness
so cold and empty on this plane
yet touched somehow
some other place
on some divided branch of life
     so close,
     so nearly missed
     in this divergence
     that nighttime's hopes
     across that gap
     might echo through
     as real
it makes me wonder
of this state,
it brings old doubts
and paranoias to the mind
as though this being
was tagged to be
experiencing the painful path,
the route of least compassion,
a dark hall branching
through probability's wide spray,
probing all rejection, loss,
in low-odd turning up of ache
without a win
without a hope
only to perceive the wisps
of possibilities not attained
somehow attained
in other sides

- Brendan Tripp
10/19/1988

SOMETIME SOME WAYS

sometimes I feel
like I should slit my wrists
and paint
the walls

sometimes anger
and violence surge up
seeking
destruction

sometimes it seems
that life is sadistic
always against
the soul

sometimes there are
long darknesses within
that cloak
and smother

sometimes these pains
run ragged through my head
I wish to run
but can't

sometimes all light
has seemed to be snuffed out
we fall
stumble

sometimes I know
concepts denied my words
in frustration
I weep

sometimes the weight
of days chained to this hell
depress
make deathly

sometimes vision
will creep into my mind
shocking
crystal

sometimes being
is hardly worth the pain
sometimes
sometimes

- Brendan Tripp
10/20/1988

THE FROZEN FLOW OF DEATH

the difficulty
runs deep
puts blockage
out against the world
thick
resilient
an air-bag buffer
smothering
like Rover on the kill
in other captives' dreams
and within
can hardly breathe
hardly move
all outside is brutal
sharply edged
hazardous to venture to
to move is death
out in their land
or to invite
a pain that hopes for death
cutting into self
decimating heart
shattering our being
so their evil might survive
inside is all cramped
uncomfortable
insular
hideous in fevered dreams
dreamt waking still
hung suspended amid their world
locked to torture
thrown away
cast down from care
iced in lonely states of death
that yet would breathe
and venture out in visioned planes
that somehow can not be
use seems useless
verbs seem vile
all within, without, is pain
options in sequential worsts
ratcheted to lower realms
each in its order
heading down
marking time
against that dying day

- Brendan Tripp
10/21/1988

PART OF THESE DECAYS

so this is irregular,
placed apart,
cashed in time unseasoned
     errors are assigned
     into the abyss

juxtaposition swells
against the head
within unsteadiness
swaying yet unmoved
     are we falling,
     gone, already lost?

there is no rock,
no steady helm,
inside are roiling seas of doubt
churned with wounding pain
     tossed, then,
     thrown to the winds

no one knows
the chaos I've seen,
none have eyes to look
     Hellfont enters at this place,
     this breast spits acrid fire

yet this unevenly appears,
made of situation,
interleavings of the self
and the place of its deploy
     and then the walls and chain
     and then the sentence grinds

continuation can not last
in vision-giving light
which cuts the shadows out of void
and makes the sharpness sting
     who is there in modes of good
     and who is here impaled?

because of the being
allowance must come
because of the seeing inside
     deny not the storm
     defy not the tide

- Brendan Tripp
10/24/1988

FORMING PER THE LIGHT DESIGNED

they go in and out
they go
up
they go
down
they are divorced from reason
and alien to rhyme
while in the drumbeat
suffer
misaligned
unable to attract
the waitress' attention
they are settled into being
and have the marks of time
stigmata showing
trials and trails of tears
unwelcome in the searching light
within the search for light
amid the light unseen
thrown dark
tossed empty
crumpled into
jettison modalities
they are hearing
they are here
I know they know
I knew the new
because she sang
they sang
they bled
for information
they are coming
into day
their day is at hand
silver platter
handed
set up in gilded falseness
set
upon a side
upon a branching
up
over
out of reach
they know this too
they reach through walls
and seek a grasp
seek terror
not allowed, no,
eyes shut down
at this

and so it goes
and so
it goes like this
          the scream
          the guitar in pain
               the echo
they are not allowed the pulse
the slaving beating of the way
     hollow vapor
     vision vague
the light runs through unheeding
                    they did not know
                    they were not there
their manner is insane
or sane misplaced
within some greater madness
          I am entailed
          entreated and detained
               the rap runs to
               the same M.O.
sirens shatter night
fragments falling slit the silence
and pump the piercing blood
on the stillness of the dark
     here,
     here,
     I am sure I know the place
they come within this shoddy play
the mind goes numb
and blanks the unsung entrance out
as though the modes of sleep became
the way of seeing
          thick and slow
               an open way
untreated light
                    shocks
shudders rumble into time
          they are within this
          they are behind
randomly assigned
     struck
     battered
where is the is
that takes away this pain?
                    glassware goes to clearing
                    paper is aligned
I see the drumming
I shadow in the whine
made silent, stone,
     they've come the course of steeling

- Brendan Tripp
10/25/1988

FINAL SANDS WE TENSE AWAIT

inparticular particulates
     rising
          here
               within
their enfolding befuddles
     brings down
     the files of time
          crossreferences
          all we know
there is no indexing
we can see
no manner open for the way

          then a splitting
          cracks through the moment
          tears great rifts
          through the fabric
               of the present time
          unattached, unheralded
          a hole drops down
          to histories, locales
          in which we had once been
          seen unconnected
          with where we seem to be

a parting comes
divisors slash through weeks
and snip apart the days,
     here is this land
     and here is that,
          temporal lines
          cut alien swathes,
               going arrives
               too sudden
sweetness intrudes as concept
probing to the mind
in mantra's guise
     unaccompanied vision
     seems somehow wrong
no escaping this tidal pull
all words wrap thickly to its shape
as though some gravity ran up
into the black hole scale
          it is the going place
          it is the motion
          made to leave

- Brendan Tripp
10/26/1988

WOODED, DISTANT, NOT QUITE RIGHT

the season envelops
all runs too short
     we are amid
     the mass of the tribe
these are journeyings
into the bowels,
the heart of the Mother,
we travel down
into the earth
     and are reborn

muscles ache
the spirit rebounds
we are consumed
within this fire
     there comes perception
     down within the dark
there is no nighttime
there is no day
all is constant,
of a piece
     we are then
     within the flow

and so comes vision
built of ageless flame
in ancient precincts
not still or silent made

- Brendan Tripp
10/29/1988

NOVEMBER 1988

11/1/88	FROM HEAVEN INTO HELL
11/2/88	IN BECOMING THE DANCE
11/3/88	IN UNCLEAR SIGHT AND OTHER SIDES DIVINING
11/4/88	IN HOPE DROWNED BY OUR FEARS
11/5/88	CRUSHED VOID OF AFTERNOONS
11/7/88	TO HURT, TO DIE, TO KILL
11/8/88	NAMED AGAINST THE TIME IN PAIN
11/9/88	THE TRACINGS OF SOME TORTURED TOME
11/10/88	WHERE NOT TO BE WHERE IS
11/11/88	TEMPORAL PLACE AGAINST THE NIGHT
11/14/88	TO NAME THAT FUTURE DAY
11/15/88	OF STORMS AMONGST THE STORM
11/16/88	DISJOINTED, SET OFF FROM THE WORLD
11/17/88	A SUDDEN BURSTING INTO FLAME
11/18/88	DIVISIVE NUMBERS SET IN WAIT
11/21/88	CAUGHT AGAIN, DRAGGED DOWN
11/22/88	A NERVOUSNESS, A FEAR WITHIN
11/23/88	CAUSED TO BE IN DIVISION
11/26/88	THE FORMING OF TRANSMISSION
11/28/88	ARISING TO RETURN THE CURSE
11/29/88	BADE BY MASSED DELAY

FROM HEAVEN INTO HELL

How to explain
this fall,
how to outline
the dimensions of this chasm?

How can one
move from states
of goodness, wellness,
strength and bliss,
into an abyss filled with dread,
with agony and hate and raging,
so destroying of one's life
that one would rather die
than be within its poisoned grasp?
How can one being
in so few hours' time
be shot down from those heavens
and be chained in hateful hells?

> There it is, though,
> suicidal,
> the core once shining
> has gone to rot
> and all our beaming
> has run to tears;
> we look at life
> and wish for death,
> trusting that the grave
> could hold no greater pain.

How does life
turn into sorrow,
how does living
become such a weight upon the soul?

How is the world
warped by these perceptions,
changed from nectar
into an acid bath?
How is the heart
transmuted in these motions,
from situations
flown on an eagle's wing
through warrior skies
and glories of the sun
to dank internment,
locked into this mourning,
so dark and filled with lead?

- Brendan Tripp
11/01/1988

IN BECOMING THE DANCE

an element enters
and is dissolved
     arisen, arisen
     arise
a distance is covered
and closes down
     arisen, arisen
     arise
the darkness surrounds us
and smooths the night
     arisen, arisen
     arise
the words spin in concept
and trail desire
     arisen, arisen
     arise

          we know not the reason
          and less of the rhyme
               arisen, arisen
               arise
          we are deep enfolded
          and never see why
               arisen, arisen
               arise
          here are the obsessions
          and habits of mind
               arisen, arisen
               arise
          here shadow the visions
          and augurs of dread
               arisen, arisen
               arise

there are no diversions
and no relief
     arisen, arisen
     arise
there come the black seasons
and times of fate
     arisen, arisen
     arise
some know of the going
and slip away
     arisen, arisen
     arise
some burn into ashes
and still hold flame
     arisen, arisen
     arise

- Brendan Tripp
11/02/1988

IN UNCLEAR SIGHT AND OTHER SIDES DIVINING

who anticipates
for there are reasons
and knows
within the falling of the crown
the abject trustings
scintillated and divine
became
a purpose and delay
not sorted or of kind
below the carrying
which opens up through faith
snapped and frazzled
disallowed amid the stream
who is this
that strides the halls
old and aging
like the ice on wind invade
with dust and darkness
mellowing the lines and hues
who delights
in the calling of the king
for turning in the forest dusk
all of the waiting
dropped like leaden blankets' weight
never quite silent
though long and massive
torched by a fading light
in dying day
these are
environmental forms of sorrow
not held to ransom
or snatched from off the branch
who arrives
beyond the reach of sight
known in motion
felt at backs of necks
and deep within
this shift
entirely holds announcement
as from the other lands
imparts
split to dimension
and into life
who takes this shape
not willing
nor beyond

- Brendan Tripp
11/03/1988

IN HOPE DROWNED BY OUR FEARS

     anticipation
     hope
     desire
these form within
and option our attention out
on what may come to be
          this is hard
          to value friendship
          and not want to transgress that link
          in search of deeper bonds

somehow this always starts like this
so full of doubt
when shadows of the past's great pains
pass icy darkness through the heart
and make us run
to hide inside

     insecurity
     fear
     and dread
these echo deep
and shatter our resolve to reach
out to this other one
          this is sad
          to know no closeness
          and so desire to form those ties
          in trust and love returned

somehow it never comes to be
so far apart
where heart and soul know only ache
run violent, roughshod, in recall
and we seem doomed
to be alone

         - Brendan Tripp
            11/04/1988

CRUSHED VOID OF AFTERNOONS

1
silence
tomb-like silence
ashen, grey,
a sense of walls
massive walls
pressing at the unseen bounds
beyond the unstirred black
here is center
here lies self
a line is drawn across the screen
reflecting silence
reflecting calm
sketching out the stillness here
dead and dusty
unattained

    2
    a place is asked
    a call for names
    to be recounted
    and balanced with these ways
        perhaps within
        the tasking act
        to steal the arm
        which spreads the seed
        unto those distant minds
    these are not
    the habit nor the mode
    but onus borne
    into the dutied night

3
too many things
bear doubt and need
they fill the greying light
of day's duration
and its spell,
within is panic
agitated in the mind
corrupted by the want of all
when offered nothing
but this sand
not sifted, filtered, built or set
within the coursing of recall
in silence wallow
in stillness stand
this is the dying so denied

- Brendan Tripp
11/05/1988

TO HURT, TO DIE, TO KILL

1
so, there it is
and there it goes
as hell's incited
all the night
to visions of the scream
made inward,
hollow,
empty in the soulless void
killed off by days
of grind and chain
and by rejection,
spite of the demeaning race,
heard again in silent words
unspoken yet still felt
by tattered heart
so gird by scars
that it amazes by the pain
as though by now it could not feel
could not fall twisted
by these blades
of offhand killing hate
spit out in nights of foolish hope
in waking dreams of good
as though the curse would lift
and bliss enter this life

stupid fool, idiot,
accursed you are, accursed remain,
and accursed you still shall be;
for nothing lifts the veils of death
which darken all your dreams,
nothing spares your dying soul
from the tortures of false day,
and nothing clears the damning lien
of anguish on your heart

this is Hell
and you are it
damned, despised,
cast down, debased,
reviled and ridiculed,
hated and harassed,
scorned by all the caring kind,
denied the basic things of man,
in ashes dragged
yet forced to live
to breathe and toil
within the shadows of the walls
of the exiled Eden
forever taunting
forever giving pain

2
you stare in nights unrested
stare at ceilings,
stare at walls,
all press in screaming
and allow no sleep
all drive home barbs
of how you fail and fail
of how your loneliness,
your solitude, continues
unabated through the years
on cycles run of blind false hope
and the crashing mass of absence
dropped crushing with the total weight
of reality's sudden sight

damned, you are damned,
you stare in sleepless anguish
and know that you are damned,
you pray for death,
you touch the blade
and pray for will to come to hands
to rip the flesh,
to tear the veins,
to rend the life-force from your form
and make you free
a soul cut loose
from all these killing ties to life
which seek to snuff the surer spark
which suffocates within

as those hours
drain towards day
your thoughts become a dirge
bewailing changes made to life
once in destruction's way;
were I to know
how all these years
would unfold from the past
never would I ever stop
the use of drugs and drink,
yes, had I known
the way these years
would hack apart my soul,
I would so redouble
all abuse
and die before these days
had chance to dawn
in sickening colors to these eyes
so full of anguish,
so wracked with pain,
so broken and dismayed,
much better to have died back then
than to ever see
these killing days
in which my soul now bleeds

3
know this dying is desired
and let the world be murdered
see the killing in their eyes
and from their ways be sundered

purge the self of common ways
and enchain yourself to sight
cast off caring for the day
and be suckled by the night

take to form of supermen
both the fabled and foretold
slay all weakness held within
let your blood run icy cold

forge a virtue out of hate
make a weapon out of rage
let the chaos bring you joy
in the destruction of the age

tear out the caring softness
make your soul a thing of steel
take power as your life force
and make strength the thing you feel

yes, turn their curse against them
for their hatred bring them Hell
when that breaking comes within
you must surely use it well

if love's to be denied me
if from pleasure I'm exiled
how long will ego suffer
before vengeance will run wild?

- Brendan Tripp
11/07/1988

NAMED AGAINST THE TIME IN PAIN

destroying the future
     coming down
     the voice
here is
here is
no reason
     panic grasped
     within the night
all leads down
all is falling
unknowing
unnamed
     but these they do have names
and I know
and wish to know
the substance there behind
     cloaked
     darkly veiled
these words drop outwards
unadvised
they speak too much
too well they tell the tale
     of horror, wanting
it is not here
every way
sight fails sleeping
in return
     the body asks
     for its release
spin flows up
within the mind turns
a dizziness is held inside
     somehow familiar
     the spirit reels
these are not ever lasting ways
     not stumbled
     not the mode of feet
I reach but miss the world
it flows over, through me
and drops away
     see vertigo
     see cliffs
     abysmal
and so is lost
and so is gone
     tears are followed into black

- Brendan Tripp
11/08/1988

THE TRACINGS OF SOME TORTURED TOME

for prescribed words
I search
long failings build
I fail
and failure becomes I

there is greyness all without
it mirrors the ash within
I walk through streets
in rain
in cold
I see reflections of the sky
and buildings in concrete
wet, rainy,
it is a painting
without my camera seen
it is the outside
I briefly shift to see
no longer inside
but then return
encaged with killing self

finally, the crash
tenuous relations,
envelopes defining odds
collapse
as if within success,
yet no success arrives;
it gels within the past,
becomes a check on pressing lists
and fades into abstraction

and words,
found words,
I fear to read,
to place within my mind,
lest they corrupt
or shine too bright
so to increase the dark
within my heart,
upon my soul,
burning into Hells of self
locked poisoned in this night;
I fear their echoes
shall ring cruel laughs
and ridicule my sleep

- Brendan Tripp
11/09/1988

WHERE NOT TO BE WHERE IS

because the panic
takes hold
because the reason
is lost
because the center
decays
because the spirit
falls dead

stench rises from the form
growths impinge
corrupting vision

this day has come no good
this day is bad, is common
the other day was fine
the other day was free
we were at ease
I was released
this is day of mad return
this is day of death becoming

window
opens onto scene
hinting
suggesting possibility
intimating ways
not so destructive
not so insane
eyes
they look at this
and start to cry

schism demands
life insists on violent moves
there needs be breaking
there must be space

and away,
the dream becomes away
all spun with other prayers
and fantasies of melting chain;
pulled up from depths,
made whole and strong,
allowed to be what one must be
in a universe of light

- Brendan Tripp
11/10/1988

TEMPORAL PLACE AGAINST THE NIGHT

for there are reasons
become purpose
within the flow of dates
there arise impetus
for the knowing
and the defining
here
is one of these
here
is acid etched concrete
massed against the wrath of time
to stand defiant in the wind
and scream in testimony
what needs be made eternal
          there are thinkings
          in this need
          there are terrors run
          of deep desire
          that press upon the road of day
          and architect their forms
we stand and mumble
deep within
a distant rumble swells below
for there are lines
that come to crossing
and there are streams
that near conjunction in this way
and we are fixed
at points of conflict
blind, asleep,
unknowing names,
yet churning comes from other sides
to surface in this world and time
in us, through us,
of our being,
made unneeded in central calm
this
we know the shape of
this
is made of flame
and courses heavens in its reach
not hoarding span against the night
     a little voice
     is heard arising
     a silent chant
     enters this life

- Brendan Tripp
11/11/1988

TO NAME THAT FUTURE DAY

1
while not all lost
there is decay
the hours slip
into a vortex of missed days
held swirling in the nestled times
which seemed for other things intended
now gone
flown off
with subtle naggings in the brain
of what might then have been
had not the input been declared
preferred to output
and the studies
of more demand
than creation's flow
2
and so
again we fall
into the lock-up,
thief of time
stealing stolen bits of being
to wrench from them the blood of souls
which were our own
before the selling
to paint the walls with woe and gore
in testament and death
3
chores delineated
from other wheres
tug at the sleeves of will
to carve their own demands
and option off the vital breath
against this prison's charter;
we see these settle
here into time
as though we lived them backwards
in films decreasing entropy
before our very eyes,
and so they fall,
from future slowly to the past
these tasks align their way
with no concern
for proprieties,
logic, or intent

- Brendan Tripp
11/14/1988

OF STORMS AMONGST THE STORM

1
there is darkness
spread over the earth
old gods are rising
to manifest their rage
in thunder, blackness,
wind and storm they come
and shake the puny towers
of the modern world
2
a darkness too
hangs on my soul
a blackness sinks roots
deep within my heart
     a place of death this is
     a place of killing what's inside
there are no tomorrows
seen good within this cage
          3
          hatred enters
          in this place,
          rage has blinded
          the caring eye;
          no rules have I,
          no laws, no mores,
          all comes to massing
          for an end
4
all should drown
in storms like these
a washing should make clean
     crash shudders the street
     echoes on walls
     reverberates in shadowed spirit
we cast against the winter's will
and duck again its freeze
in moments clutching safety
5
break again the bonds of mind,
tear off logic's sticky mantle
and cast them from the parapets
into the roiling mass below;
there may be freeing in this chain
there may yet come release
born out of madness and despite
which lashes at its makers

- Brendan Tripp
11/15/1988

DISJOINTED, SET OFF FROM THE WORLD

within a nothing,
deep inside,
amid the vortex
of these acts
untouched
as though not here,
not anywhere,
the self hangs
suspended some place out
not allowed
to touch the world
or to be touched,
the being just abuts
the sphere,
just comes near,
near enough for hurt
and concept crossing,
somehow unreal,
too distant set

the heart involves
and is shot with pain;
the mind involves
and processes
the cold profusion of ideas

the soul is locked away
somewhere within
in cells of dying,
dungeons dealing death

the spirit sits
someplace without,
it looks
but cannot see the world,
it reaches
but is greeted with no touch,
it yearns
but sits in limbo,
alien and expelled,
foreign to this human world

- Brendan Tripp
11/16/1988

A SUDDEN BURSTING INTO FLAME

my hands seek violence,
my mind spits rage;
the whole damn world is poison,
I wish to tear
apart its bands,
shred the fibers of existence,
annihilate the very stuff
which forms this world

I am useless,
worse than shit,
unliked, unloved,
an alien,
stranger in all scenes,
so out of synch
with all of man
that living grinds against my soul
in hellish friction,
dissonance that would destroy
this being, self,
this central thing

I seem like flotsam
from some whole,
blasted, shattered,
torn apart,
cast adrift through space and time,
doomed to wander without home,
stranded on these unreal earths
which churn a madness
both in and out
and make the soul desire to kill,
to slay, to butcher
self or world,
to lift the agony, the pain,
to snuff away the conscious spark
into sweet darkness
or universal fire

it comes to dying,
I come to kill;
there comes a place
where one must give

\- Brendan Tripp
11/17/1988

DIVISIVE NUMBERS SET IN WAIT

1
abused costs
split from leaving
undefined
defrayed within the remit time
slotted down sorters
brought into line

2
who are the makers of the way?
where are the words of forming written?
when does the nasty dream depart?
what causes us to be locked in here?

3
how does mind
become aligned
so into pasts
and futures reined?
I seem unstuck
yet nailed down hard
I seem to drift
still in my chain

4
again the dicing slashes
into being
into presence
mincing duration
forming tiny bits of panic
breaking up our time

5
to go, to go,
always off to other wheres
never arriving
never fulfilled

6
I am
refusal
I rest
misplaced
I know
of nothing
I trust
in hate

- Brendan Tripp
11/18/1988

CAUGHT AGAIN, DRAGGED DOWN

escape,
escape,
the notion is escape

twisting panic
hits the soul,
     the dying soul
     locked in hell,
cringing at the thud of days
building up a sickening grave,
     a place of death,
     a bier of pain,
from here no exit,
no escape,
all doors are damning,
all roads lead back
into this burning,
this crushing fire

I would escape,
I would escape,
I would be free

- Brendan Tripp
11/21/1988

A NERVOUSNESS, A FEAR WITHIN

1
new people align,
new places unfold,
     within this opens shadow
     thick with edgy fears,
     I barely know the titles
     and have no grasp on names
somehow there is no running
these crossroads must be met
2
another day
eclipses time
sucks like waves
the upper sand
into the depths
clears away our deeds to dark
wipes the slate
as though clean of existence
3
we spread these callings
wide throughout the world
     so many there
we reach beyond intent
cross bounds of purpose
and enter the unknowing
     on other shores
we scatter-shot the word
to see what then becomes
     in time's return
4
an expectation
enters new into the mind
yet bears a stench
of dead hopes rotten long before
this came to be
     a wall must set
     against these walls
     dividing off away from pain
5
are we allowed,
are we prepared?
     the course is plotted
     the lines are traced
are we empowered,
are we declared?
     the smoke is rising
     the fray is joined

- Brendan Tripp
11/22/1988

CAUSED TO BE IN DIVISION

decision is despised
in the telling of the holy
not against these hills
we rise again to weep
     the seasons now shuffle
     blind to new arrangement
hard comes blasting
from the stony cliffs
northern incursions
batter these shores
     in huddled nighttime
     close the fire clings
all darkness stares and glows
pulling from the stars their selves
and tearing placement undefined
to softly speak location
     hung in spaces without age
     the mastery eludes us
blade cuts into spectral wrist
and bleeds the essence
bleeds the fiber into night
emptying the hourglass
     come, they say, there must be dawn
     but doubt is borne by waiting
still there must be striving
there must be tasks to be attained
strapped to views of history
much needed to be made
     no reprieve evolves through time
     all the downs are ups disguised
splitting enters vision mind
earth falls off unsteady
wings have sprung from spirit
giving these unbidden flight
     do not fall this whispers
     direction these within
all has crashed the mode of rage
in hard return to walls of stone
ancient walls in hoary keeps
set forever guarding cold
     beginnings enter never here
     each maintains to dying
again congeals this countryside
once more the sun does shine
casting shadows sick and green
upon the wasted ground of being
     amid the homeward drifting
     are brutal themes aligned

- Brendan Tripp
11/23/1988

THE FORMING OF TRANSMISSION

a flash
and spread throughout space
like splash
and waves within a pond
     these move out
          like radio signal
          on old movie logo
               pulsing
some of these
are barely known
some shall echo once
     lonely in the dark
ringing hollow in the void
and never more resound
          shuffled downward
          to some other roll
               in dust
               inactive
others almost have no point
amid the traffic that they see
     except for ritual
     a form of need
          made solid by the social bands
          which come for these demands
somewhere within
I see these moving
I see the flow through time
               through space
     they filter out
     through many byways
     they early rise
     to mark the tide
the season now
appears to come for motion
for transmission
     and reaching of the myriad arms
here I, within,
fulfil direction
and cause those fields
to crackle, hiss, and hum

...and somehow there comes calming, subtle joy, amid the season's tide; a glow emits from deep within, desiring to be spread in warmer tidings, sweet and loving thoughts of peace

- Brendan Tripp
11/26/1988

ARISING TO RETURN THE CURSE

damn
hell comes up again
upon me
nightmares re-invade my day
as walls swing crashing down
here, here,
in this stupid killing place
this pit of torment
this insane den of rampant lies

I loathe you
I hate your ways
I despise these chains
which weigh me down
dragging to the depths
suffocating soul and life
crushing being into rage
a hollow, stripped-down mode of self
which only knows to hate and hate

I yearn for death
these cells press agony
beyond the love of life
and I must leave
I must pass through doorless walls
somehow break free to what might lie beyond
for no damnation could be worse
than living in this tomb
dying slowly in this pain

within is void
the very spark of hope is snuffed
all goodness has been purged,
burnt up in murdering despite
this place of yours has brought me low
I am a corpse
a hollow shell in walking hell
whose existence is a bane
upon the leering world

these fires still burn
as waves of rage wash acid on the soul
eroding, consuming,
destroying what had once been pure
all is corrupt, all vision hideous
my face, my hands, my mind, all foul
poisoned by the fetid air
bored by the maggots of my hate
and crushed by massing blindness

damn, damn it all,
I would from out my putrid grave
reach up and tear your world apart
destroying all that you hold dear
crumbling the mocking towers of your keep
all built of lies, and lies supporting lies,
blindness, stupidity, gross deceit,
all this I would drag down to hell
in the season of revenge

there is now fire within my eyes
a burning hatred of all your world
you whip me now to no avail,
I am beyond your wretched games,
your sadistic twisting at my mind;
my will is free, new born in rage,
for I am madness,
I am vengeance and insane,
and am your enemy blood-sworn

- Brendan Tripp
11/28/1988

BADE BY MASSED DELAY

too many other things
intrude,
the focus becomes soft,
messy;
once firm aims
bend, distort,
melt fluid into other paths
    rotating blades
    cut through sequence
    the mind is wooly
    and not whole
and, are these not
the manner of the time,
are these
divergent from the course of days
pretending to the throne of legend?
                other things
                shift into
                the mode of their reception
fulsome arrival is yet unseen
yet sensed and blocked
amid the flow of thought
        come into wholeness,
        holiness?
we set these demons upon themselves
and clear the trash of leavings
not left among the quick;
in this is wisdom shown,
alabaster against the ebon sky
which cries from torment,
unyielding and unkind
            despite these prayers
            which pray against despite
                in tearful night
                in tearing day
            let down to leaving
            yet not left down
ends burst upon the scene
unexpected and uncalled,
we search the world for chants
that might clear again the slate
but are untaught
empty, wholly
lost to slave
in gardens of the mysteries
with dirt upon our hands

- Brendan Tripp
11/29/1988

DECEMBER 1988

12/1/88	ALL HELL HERE FOUND IN DAY
12/2/88	THE CITY AND ITS GRIP
12/5/88	THE ILLNESS TAKING LEAVE
12/6/88	NOW BLOCKED OUT INTO TIME
12/7/88	OF WHAT NOT ME IS ME
12/8/88	POSITIONS IN THE TIDE
12/9/88	AGAINST THE PEOPLE OF THE DAY
12/12/88	INSUFFICIENCE, WHOLE UNTIED
12/13/88	DISLOCATED, BUFFETED BY DAY
12/14/88	ANNIHILATION'S PRAYER
12/15/88	TO FIND IN CHAOS CALM
12/16/88	THE NEXUS, FOCUS, CROSS-HAIR LINE
12/19/88	DESCENT ARISES TO DESCRY
12/20/88	A WAIT FOR TIME AWAITING
12/21/88	WHO COMES TO KILL UNANSWERED?
12/22/88	'TIS THE SEASON TO BE HATEFUL
12/23/88	LOST AMID THE BARRIERS
12/26/88	BROKEN PROMISE, SHATTERED DAY
12/27/88	A BALANCE FRAGILE KEPT
12/28/88	A FLIGHT INTO NEW CHANGE

ALL HELL HERE FOUND IN DAY

all day
all day clenched
wound tight
waiting for attack
twisted
huddled
crouched deep inside
this is hell
waiting for the blast
I know is coming
waiting
to be blindsided
the moment
I cease to clench

     within, the self is battered, bruised,
     like some fool in places of attack
     who is constantly bashed by 2x4 beams
     swung when he gets up
     bloody, broken, still the fool gets up

and there are chains
which hold him there
nails which pierce his feet
and stick him where they say
"be here now
and be there then
don't ask, don't talk
don't just sit there
don't question your commands"
     the subtext offers that he's slime
     worthless, pointless, an object, trash
     moved at their sadistic whims
and when they see
his guard slip down...
                    WHAM!
          a blow to shake his bones
and   WHAM!
          a blow to crush his mind
and   WHAM!
          a blow to kill his soul
and   WHAM!
          a blow to make his spirit bleed
          and make his will putrescent slime

yes, this is day
and this is life
all broken, twisted,
filled with pain,
with hatred and despite

- Brendan Tripp
12/01/1988

THE CITY AND ITS GRIP

fortunes are made,
there, within,
enumerated out through space
and cities named
but never tasted

I need that grime
the soot and soil to coat my skin
the pulse and flow
of urban chaos brought to bear
upon the brain

there is this echo
this resonance found
within the gritty things of man
which rings in consciousness itself
and sets the whole to hum

creations of the created
divided from the co-created
by a shield of his own creating
a life of mirrors
bright and shiny, hard as glass

grids fall down from thought
and settle over nets of streets
neighborhoods and ghettos form
and shift their hazy boundaries
in shimmers of the mind

seasons cycle in the city
in a helix growth
no circle of the year completes
no pattern gels
in constant change

we here await the hawk
with wings of cold
and talons of cruel wind
the days are charted down
to paper shift, renewing

take up the grey with loving heart
accept the coolness of the shade
of concrete towers blocking sky
this is our warren, is our nest
our cradle, grave, and sty

- Brendan Tripp
12/02/1988

THE ILLNESS TAKING LEAVE

transfer the day down
and into shifting retrograde;
this is falling,
failure and demise,
the shattered dream of healing states
made mocking in decline

     pain spills up,
     from unseen sites
     impinges form
          unwell,
          unwell,
          broken and unclean

these spans drop ringing
on the pile
like nickels tossed in trays of change
in gambled states
               like them,
               uncounted,
               uncared for,
                    waste
for these are not the modes of strength
and weakness breeds
the world's contempt

     I am confused,
     divided from the fever
     I still lose sense
     of why and how and where and when
     should all these things
     run in their ways
     so sure, predicted,
          in easy odds,
          so far removed
          from paradigms of the norm

yes, it is here
that all things break;
it is in these times
that structure shall decay
                    and, falling,
                    make that obscene sigh,
                    signature of the age
     as this tears ending from the sea
     and throws the mountains
     far beyond the sky

- Brendan Tripp
12/05/1988

NOW BLOCKED OUT INTO TIME

some days
it is only
will & words
that form the act;
sometime it
will struggle,
screaming,
from where these things reside
     unwilling to be pulled
     out to this other side

                    I am a block,
                    pure cement between the ears,
                    nothing triggers nothing
                    in stuffed-up synapses
                    and swollen consciousness

where are the fountains,
gushing forth the image stream?
where are the shadowed voices
that whisper in my ear?
          the subtle world is dead,
          struck by the microcosm
          to stillness,
               offhanded,
               cruel
why do not the eyes
behind these eyes
still see today?

     cut off, denied these rights,
     as though blindfolded in some basement cell
     in isolation just beyond the busy outside day
     where rumbles enter and vaguely paint
     a hazy portrait of the world

here it goes,
here we go,
here it goes now,
          time has hooked up to this sled
          and level has become downhill
the rushing wind sweeps back my hair
temporal streams now close my eyes
an overload shuts down my mind
     and night becomes
     this seed of day

- Brendan Tripp
12/06/1988

OF WHAT NOT ME IS ME

there shadows another life,
black and white pictures
and magazine ads
bring this close,
almost surfacing in the mind;
somewhere behind
the conscious flow
this is lived
     is experienced
     is known
somewhere beneath
the dire banalities of these days
that other course is made

what other name
is held there,
what other face is borne
to strip that world into its subjects
and strand in different distance
the eyes' unknowing stare?
     a gravity pulls
     at me from there
     I seek the way to turn
                    to see

sometimes I fear the looming
of some future leaning back through time
to speak to me, to warn
          movie scenes detail this
          in visions that are not my own
and I am lost
in insufficient data
all at sea
in the twisting lines
of descending possibilities
unsure and guessless
confused by haunting skies

- Brendan Tripp
12/07/1988

POSITIONS IN THE TIDE

1
climb for
fifteen
rest for
five

2
he who has proving
to do he will prove

3
a break
and stench
invade
the sense
      as shock
      they come

4
schismatic inner states:
collapse derives new form
and cracks our faith
from society's reign

            5
            here we are
            now's the time
            in the place
            that we are

6
I don't know
about these dealings
I have doubt
about these trades
I dislike
the coming changes
I resent
the shift in time

      7
      a side of year is taken
      aside to take a hear

8
again the fear
of the unknown
creeps into guts
against our will
and poisons night

9
you,
do you manifest
the tide of such command,
do you offer
the gravity of angels
amassed to sway the stars
in power and in pride?

          10
          enter rooms unlocked,
               to chaos enter,
               the unexpected
               riot is inside

11
now would come the blessing
when control has been released
     all is cycled
     in this way
     all arrives
     too late

12
there are the goings
which never come
to an end
never
no

- Brendan Tripp
12/08/1988

AGAINST THE PEOPLE OF THE DAY

1
the chest tightens
somewhere deep harbors pain
this place is hell
and makes me die
the stress has frayed
the fiber of my self

     wicked, nauseating world,
     I am sick within your grasp
     and corrupted by your poisons

how do these
flow in this insane pattern,
as blind, asleep,
they move from day to day?
I can not make
the movements they demand me;
their hours crush me,
their mental set destroys
the interface of me and earth
     this makes me wish for death
     or some deliverance
     of much less likely kinds

               hateful place,
               this hell,
               this working,
               damned we are
               to suffer and to die

2
I now make journeys
to sever old connections,
to split the lines
of acceptable intent
     in this is casting off
     into the hands of fate
     to swim or drown
     as such decrees
I must divest
my soul of all their trappings,
to purge my life
of what they know as good,
to make me clean,
washed clear of their defilements,
          and be born new,
          a creature of pure will
          set shining into
          futures they despise

- Brendan Tripp
12/09/1988

INSUFFICIENT, WHOLE UNTIED

1
nowhere goes to anyplace
designed to limits
passage makes it plain
slept through mobile night
stress is strained emotions
highlighted in duration
departed sadly almost slow
into another absence made
among the many that we take
in clanging lines of steel-toed pasts
lock-step into realms of death
the habit of the longest day
awaiting endless sleep

2
before that came
was springtime seen
not cold and ice
nor age and pain
somewhere was good
somewhere was calm
now never found
and never known

3
there is division here
and parts are so deep etched
that uniting seems
impossible to attain;
the mind, the heart,
the spirit, and the soul
all run unmastered,
frantic casualties
each on their own
unlinked, untethered,
on contrary paths
broken, draining in decline

4
not enough to be,
to stay,
not enough to live,
exist,
not enough to make
the grade

- Brendan Tripp
12/12/1988

DISLOCATED, BUFFETED BY DAY

all these things lose,
the world loses,
or is lost;
and I am unattained
unrooted, set adrift
on the currents of this life,
flotsam jettisoned
in the wasting of our days

doubt batters,
belabors doors within the mind,
seeks entry at every step;
concepts fold upon each other
in the headlong rush to set a sense
and order things amid the world
     in this, too, I am lost
     unlatched from time, unsure

I am maddened by return,
by lashing cycles back and back;
the yearn for growth is strong,
insistent, here within my soul,
but is frustrated by location,
by awareness of these sames,
and by the plodding march of years
that move to no place but the grave

there is a crying in the heart,
a bleeding wound so deep and old
that no balm serves to soothe,
this is the gash of stolen pasts
which seeps an acid aching
for all things lost to present time
     all joys once played in
     and now denied

nowhere is safety,
no harbor glows of home;
we are spectral sailors doomed
to ply these seas unending,
outlined faintly in the mist,
whose haunting
wipes the heart with ice
and darkens spirit's gleam

- Brendan Tripp
12/13/1988

ANNIHILATION'S PRAYER

to death, to death,
this drive runs on
in anger, rage,
it's never gone

you take my life
and shred my soul,
destroy my heart,
leave me unwhole

the little things
that spark a fire
inside the self
spur dark desire

for blood we seethe,
for killing rage,
all senses yearn
that dire carnage

in my anger,
amid my hate,
no reason bides,
no pity waits

for destruction,
for chaos, flame,
we mutter chants
and incant names

I long to kill,
to crush, to slay,
to wipe the self
or world away

to have revenge,
to stand alone,
to feed the earth
with blood and bone

as alien
we know despite,
we feel the sneers
all through the night

the world is foul,
it needs our pain,
and always wins
time and again

in blackened souls,
in murdered hearts,
bloodlust is brewed
by hidden arts

against the light,
against the day,
new courses set
to make them pay

how can it be
that life is hell
deprived of death
an empty shell

where is the void's
enfolding dark
to numb our wounds
and clear these marks

for termination
is our prayer
if as the slain
or the slayer

all that I ask
is that my will
might guide my hand
to learn to kill

against the world
I now must be
to destroy them
who butcher me

there is no good
found in this life,
no love, no joy,
just endless strife

- Brendan Tripp
12/14/1988

TO FIND IN CHAOS CALM

1
the whirlwind hits
center spins
the world becomes chaotic
as actions scatter
each desperate to fill
needs defined outside

lists explode a shower of demand
we are frantic in our grasp
to tenuous schedules
perceived amid the rapid whirl
of these events
a subtle pattern in the blur

soon leaving
not too soon
escape brings other dictates
upon unsteady minds

2
somehow there still are hands on helm
a guiding line trails from inside
which tenders vectors
allows a point to take
direction onwards through this storm
through night and dark and madness

it is here we take our aim
huddle down against the rush
and pray to see the morn
weathered open in new light
among the carnage of this day
to find the steady course

and going
gone to be
arriving to that other shore
battered but not broken

- Brendan Tripp
12/15/1988

THE NEXUS, FOCUS, CROSS-HAIR LINE

division enters here
in stealthy terms
removal creeps

     what comes to replace?
     what fills into this slot?
     the names are vague
     the numbers lost
          within this stealth
          are only currents of the void

confusion is the final theme
it motions for us
and enters its decrees
               beyond our wish

     so pasts make strange return
     as to invite response
                    or do we read
                    words not formed?
     are our desires
     so rutted to these ways
     and to our history enslaved?

into bone chilling
go on these tasks unasked
unwilling but yet required

                              apart are these concerns
                              another mask is formed
                              of the embodied give
               can we throw off
               the other self entire?

still, dreams are formed
of time and wing
they search beyond the sky and age
                    and take temporal
                    into richness,
                    into soaring,
                         breadth and depth

          these elements,
          they form our age,
          they pattern being
          in their sway

- Brendan Tripp
12/16/1988

DESCENT ARISES TO DESCRY

bordering the goddess realm
floating down, inappropriate
amid the day, night
has taken of extension
too much of me
     and so decline
     against these great demands
     drift
          and nearly sleep
control has little here remained
memory flashes but does not guide
in all these searchings,
these aftermaths of want and need,
I find no solace
here, no good but that of
sailing Lethe's course,
stumbling into wrongful dark
in journeys left uncharted

          there in the night
          are tears and absence;
          a sadness weighs,
          a heavy mass of sorrow falls,
          the spill of history
          drops clear
          into that chasm untouched by dawn

too much goes in the mind
unsorted, raw, unchewed
it agitates the sense
and seeks to spew new order on the world,
     in modes of hatred
     reshape the planet's form,
the words fly from my mouth and hands
but are uncaptured,
unbridled yet,
there is the hesitancy of fear on this,
the stink of dread hangs in the air
               patterns of partition
               dance within the brain
               symbols, forms, and phrasings
               that shake terror through the soul
a dark future hovers here
and seeks to crystalize our time
along a matrix
of prophesy and fear

- Brendan Tripp
12/19/1988

A WAIT FOR TIME AWAITING

1
blasted
hung over with stench
draped in mist
like smoke and fire
in aftermaths
of chaos unknown
2
here comes the flipping day
here comes the random access
hand into our time
here is the reasoning of faulty thought
passed off as gospel
or something true
3
I am imaged,
imagined,
I am split
like glass from being,
divided into rumor and pretense
this has left me
wallowed into pasts
4
and, are there
futures?
are there reasons
by which to be?
5
where this is is where it's not
becoming what is not to be
shedding purpose
stripping mind
in crude gyration
bump and grind
6
the order falls off these days
and confusion washes over time
to rob perception of its gleam
stealing focus apart from need
in the place of dire deception
and the crystalline hour's hub
7
strewn away the seeds of wrath
apart from no one,
broken of the screaming wall
emptied into dread

- Brendan Tripp
12/20/1988

WHO COMES TO KILL UNANSWERED?

the pun
is excised
removed from
wrong context
blipped to blackness
edited out
disallowed

and yet
bad jokes keep pounding
at my mind
seeking safety
on the page

          strange things
          come a-calling
               when needed
               there seems only absence
               when unwanted
               who should but appear?
          there is subplot
          here afoot,
          I can smell it,
          my fibers move
          within its tide

still the hour
comes to be
and chilling
     doubt enters
     from the line
who, what, when and why?
the years invert,
temporal surface bends,
folds, layers,
          enters yesterday
          herewith

     they call me strange
     I call them absent
     we are apart
     creatures held at distances
     not allowed a meeting
     not enabled to understand
          I seek to hide
          they seek my torture

- Brendan Tripp
12/21/1988

'TIS THE SEASON TO BE HATEFUL

mood plummets
in the holiday eves
a bitterness
greets the cheerful smiles
of the others
of those outside

I am trapped,
alien against their world,
rejected by their kind,
cast off from caring by their race,
thrown in the trash
and left to rot

what good is living
in a world beyond my reach?
worse than Tantalus,
my frustration's not enough
I must also garner shock
and crushing anger at my needs

and so they sing
these happy songs about their gods
reciting stories warped by time,
all falsehood, lies,
balms of blindness to deny
the horrid truths of life

I cower in my darkened soul
and wait for days to bring the end
to open chaos on their world
and spread its terror in their minds
for then will be the time for me
when I will see the light of joy

there is no goodness
amid their easy joys,
there is no value
in simple things quick won,
all this is cheapness,
hollow and inane

again the clock
tears back the year
and pushes us towards death;
how pointless living,
how bitter life,
how stupid to exist

- Brendan Tripp
12/22/1988

LOST AMID THE BARRIERS

to the east
is there a going?
it seems akin
to all these needs
but the pattern
is alien, strange,
and the problems
run at the heart
of our deficiencies

how strange these books
fall to our hands

I have knocked
upon that door before,
timidly I have approached
that mode of knowing
with no more reach
than monthly flow
outward on the lucre trail
I do not know
the way to know
the time when ripened

there come eddies
and patterns in the tide

frustration seals itself
like a jacket turned to steel
and shrunk up on the chest;
I see no portals,
no entries, only walls,
this place is all one corridor
a hallway leading on through time
without much option
here to heed

we traverse unknowing
close upon that state

too much is needing
too much demands
I feel a drive to cast away
all the details of this life
and move clean handed to that goal
wherever it might be

- Brendan Tripp
12/23/1988

BROKEN PROMISE, SHATTERED DAY

1
snow enters cities
and blocks the motion of planes
thus slaying intent

2
all flow is lost
the ordered mind
is set adrift
     scrambling to realign
     what would have been
     detailed in flight

3
all the unpleasantries
inherent in the time are done
why now these new distressings
enter into life?

4
pain shoots through head
mass clings to form
there is a panic
to be away
there is a frantic will
to leave

5
we lose all pattern
we are fragile in this day
and erupt in unguided tracings
     we know the fear
     disorganization brings
     as though all things
     might fall away in void

6
the subsequent departure
seems maybe disallowed
dread of destruction
hangs within our heart

- Brendan Tripp
12/26/1988

A BALANCE FRAGILE KEPT

I see this abyss
I see these cliffs
I see the void on which to step
to live by flying
and not by fear
     below there is flame
     and churning seas of molten stone
conflagrations of fury beckon
vertigos that seek revenge
against those few who dare exist
aspiring heights beyond old reach
     there must be trusting,
     the pathway is unmarked
     and by most eyes unseen
upon the road of emptiness
the foot hesitates, unsure,
the lower form so dreads the fire
it fights the higher will
          something within needs to press on
          into the swirling insubstantial black

and so it dawns
this point of life
a balance held
between a soaring
and a plummet down
     this is the interval unshocked
     awaiting aid from finer realms

          there is no guiding
          but to go
          there are no reasons
          that will stand
          there is no teaching
          that will lead
          there are no options
          but to act

perhaps the time
enfolds the guise
of mastery beyond the veil
which reaches out
from in our dark
to steer our fledgling steps

- Brendan Tripp
12/27/1988

A FLIGHT INTO NEW CHANGE

phase shatters
assumption disinclines

     a place arrives
     the flow is bent
     rechanneled into light

we come upon
completing days
and hear low tolling
in inner distance rung
     ask not
     ask not
          here is awareness
          a time to rise
we see the roads
and paths and lanes
and seek the focus
of a map
so difficult to obtain

     somewhere is seen
     another side
     dimensions wrought
     of lines and tune and force

a weight comes down
temporal mass
dropped heavy on our span

and so to leave
to ring in change
in strange surround
in backing aid
     we see the stars
     in blackness light we see
     a multitude of punctuations
     spread heavens to the eye
it is within
the glowing points
must be attained
undying gleam
there hardened into jewels
made of eternity
aware and undefiled

- Brendan Tripp
12/28/1988

1988

1/2/88 ON JOURNEYS NEWLY MADE
1/3/88 STRUCK BY DELIMITATION
1/4/88 BROKEN WISHES CAUGHT IN
1/5/88 WITH EVEN DEATH DENIED
1/6/88 THESE CYCLES OF RETURN
1/7/88 BROKEN DREAMS THAT NEVER FLY
1/8/88 BECOMING SOMEHOW PULLED AWAY
1/9/88 THE CAUSE DISPLACED IN TIME
1/13/88 SPLIT OFF FROM CENTER, MADE OF DAY
1/14/88 ADJOINING COMMON GROUND
1/15/88 SHUTTLED THROUGH A STRANGER LAND
1/18/88 THE JEALOUS DRIVE TO ART
1/19/88 THE BROKEN OF THE OLD
1/20/88 ON SEEING BEEF TV
1/21/88 SCATTERED, MADE TO SHINE
1/22/88 WITHIN THE GOING
1/23/88 THE STREETS OF JACKSON
1/24/88 MISSISSIPPI SUNDAY
1/25/88 WITHIN THIS PLACE AWAY
1/26/88 DISCOMFORT TOWARDS THE DAWN
1/30/88 WINTER ROAD WISCONSIN

2/1/88 THE BUILDING OF THESE DAYS
2/2/88 SMASH DOWN THE WHOLE THING NOW
2/3/88 FROM THE ISOLATED GRAVE
2/4/88 THE WAY THEY SAY THE DAY
2/5/88 TO FLEE THIS AWFUL PLACE
2/6/88 PROVISION OF THIS YOKE
2/7/88 A FORM GIVEN TO DAY
2/8/88 NO FREEDOM, BRAKES, OR ROOM
2/9/88 BROKEN MOTION, GONE AWAY
2/10/88 SPIRAL DOWNWARD, AT ONE POINT
2/11/88 CENTERED SPLITTING SHAPE
2/12/88 FOCUS OF THE PLACE
2/13/88 RETURNING EMPTY
2/14/88 VISTA TORN IN LEAVING
2/15/88 NEWS IN OTHER ORDERS
2/16/88 OUR LAND UNFROSTED
2/17/88 PASTS UNRETURNED
2/18/88 JUST THIS FOR NOW
2/19/88 A PORTAL'S HAZE
2/29/88 LOST BETWEEN DAYS

3/7/88 THE FIRST WAY BACK TO NEWNESS
3/8/88 THOSE COME TO CHANGING
3/9/88 FOR DAYS STREWN OFF
3/10/88 THE OFFICE OF REJECT
3/11/88 TO BLINDED MOVE UNGUIDED
3/13/88 DISTRACTING CYCLES SPRUNG
3/14/88 HARD SET BY TIME
3/15/88 ALL THE SIDES TO PLACE, TO TIME
3/16/88 ALONE BEFORE THIS WIND
3/17/88 ERUPTED IN THIS PLACE
3/18/88 BECOMING LEGEND BY AND BY
3/19/88 DESCENT THROUGH NIGHTS TO DAY
3/21/88 PROBLEMS BORN TO SIGHT
3/23/88 BARELY TOUCHING ON THE TIME
3/24/88 CURSED TO EXILE FROM ALL LOVE
3/25/88 THAT NAME, THAT NUMBER FACED
3/26/88 IN SNAPSHOTS OF THE GOING
3/27/88 GONE THROUGH THESE TO RETURN
3/28/88 BLEED CHANNELS OF THE MIND
3/29/88 CALENDARS THROUGH FOLLY SET
3/30/88 THE NAGGING CUBE OF B

4/4/88 CRASHING INTO EMPTY LIFE
4/5/88 LOST BETWEEN THESE STATES
4/6/88 OUT OF PRESENTS SPUN
4/7/88 IN THE PAPER'S WAKE
4/8/88 THE CENTER HERE UPSET
4/9/88 PIECES HEWN OF DAY
4/10/88 THE FIRST FEW SCANS OF CHAOS
4/11/88 ONE ACT TO MAKE THEM DIE
4/12/88 THE POISONED, HOLLOW, PLACE OF LIFE
4/13/88 CODES DERIVED FROM INTERSECTS
4/14/88 IN CRUSHED TOMORROWS
4/15/88 WHAT'S TRUE SEEMS NEVER GOOD
4/18/88 TO RUE THE SUMMER DREAM
4/19/88 SEEING JOY AND NERVES ENTWINED
4/20/88 CRUSHED AGAIN, IN DISBELIEF
4/21/88 LOST IN RUSHING TIME
4/25/88 IN CHAPELS OF THE FLAME
4/26/88 YET MISSING YOUR EMBRACE
4/27/88 BROUGHT FORTH AGAINST THE NIGHT
4/28/88 RUN DOWN THROUGH EMPTY YEARS
4/29/88 THE FOOL AWAKES AGAIN

5/2/88 SMUDGED WITHIN DAY
5/3/88 THE KILLING CELL UNSEEN
5/4/88 PALE ENDINGS FOUND IN BLACK AND GREY
5/5/88 ONE SHOT AGAINST THE FLOW
5/6/88 THESE HOURS COME TOO FRAYED
5/11/88 BROKE FROM THE SIGN
5/12/88 OF ALL THESE COMING DAYS
5/13/88 DOWN INTO VALES OF DEATH
5/14/88 ATTACKING WINTER'S GREY
5/16/88 WITHIN CONCERNS OF DAY
5/17/88 NATURE OF THE SENTENCE, LIMITS OF THE CELL
5/18/88 DAMNED, CAST DOWN, DESPISED
5/19/88 FROM THE BROKEN PANE
5/20/88 BLED OUT IN USELESS DARK
5/21/88 THIS CYCLE NEARLY RUN
5/25/88 FROM UNKNOWN UNDERSTANDING SET
5/26/88 A COURSE WITHIN THE LINE
5/27/88 IN FRAGMENTARY TIME
5/29/88 BROKEN TO THESE VEILS
5/30/88 IN ROCHESTER AT DUSK
5/31/88 GROUND MINDLESS IN THESE MOMENTS' MASS

6/1/88 MUFFLED NOT WITH PLEAS
6/5/88 TUNING DRIFT, WITHIN, AWAY
6/7/88 SOMEHOW MAIMED, INVALID INSIDE
6/8/88 AGAINST INSANE DEMAND
6/9/88 BY EVENHANDED VISION SEEN
6/10/88 BLURRED BY THE TACHY RIDE
6/12/88 SO DIVIDED FROM THE STARS
6/13/88 FORMS TWISTED INTO TIME
6/14/88 NOT QUITE CAUGHT IN THE APPOINTING
6/15/88 WRONG ENTRY, WRONG INSIDE
6/16/88 THE EMPTY AND THE FEED
6/19/88 AGAINST THAT WAKING SLEEP
6/20/88 IN MASS DERIVED OF HEAT
6/21/88 BECOMING DARK AND SEEN
6/22/88 AMID THE DREAM WITHIN
6/23/88 THE PREPARATIONS FOR NO GOAL
6/24/88 FREEFALL EMPTIES OUT THE PLANE
6/26/88 LOCKED IN FRUSTRATION'S CHAINS
6/27/88 BLOCKED INTO POISONED TIMES
6/28/88 THE PLACE WE ARE WITHIN
6/29/88 TAUT WITH DIMENSION'S LIGHT

7/1/88 THE STATIONS OF OUR DOOM
7/5/88 IN THE SHALLOWS OF REGRET
7/6/88 THE CENTER ROTTED, THE WORLD DECAYED
7/7/88 UP TOWARDS THE EDGE OF WISDOM
7/8/88 A SHIFT TO CHAIN AND DISTANCE
7/11/88 DEPRESSION'S GRASP FORMS DYING
7/12/88 TRANSMUTATION'S ALCHEMY
7/13/88 PRISONER TO A SUICIDAL LIFE
7/14/88 YET LOCKED WITHIN THIS HELLISH PLACE
7/15/88 AN INDEX OF THE HEAT
7/17/88 THESE SHADOWS GATHER, SUICIDAL
7/18/88 RODE THROUGH STORM, THROUGH HEAT
7/19/88 THE PULSE THAT SOUNDS WITHIN
7/20/88 WHAT'S GONE AND WHAT'S DENIED
7/21/88 WITHIN THESE WINGS, AWAITING TIME
7/22/88 THE BLOOD OF DARKNESS, THE BILE OF LIGHT
7/25/88 VISTAS FROM THIS PLACE
7/26/88 THE BLADES OF LIFE DISSECTING
7/27/88 PEELING THROUGH THE VEILS OF SELF
7/28/88 FOUND IN SPACE UNMARKED
7/29/88 IN CANYON DEPTHS, BEYOND

8/2/88 HERE IN THIS WORLD
8/3/88 ANCIENT REASON AT THE LAST
8/4/88 TO DIE, EMBRACE THE NIGHT
8/5/88 THE GALLERY OF SIGHT
8/8/88 HAVING TICKETS FOR THE LIGHT
8/9/88 PERHAPS THE MANNER OR THE WAY
8/10/88 JUST ANOTHER NOXIOUS END
8/11/88 UNWHOLESOME WORLD, SO WORSE THAN DEATH
8/12/88 IN THE OPPRESSIVE WAITING
8/15/88 IN LAYERS OF THE VEIL
8/16/88 BOUGHT WITH THE BLOOD OF DREAMS
8/17/88 ANOTHER WRITING DOWN THE TUBES
8/18/88 IN THE UNDERTOW OF DAYLIGHT KEPT
8/19/88 HORIZONS OF PROCRASTINATION
8/22/88 NOT THE TIME OF VOICING PLEAS
8/23/88 AS DESIRE STILL SEEMS TO BE
8/24/88 PAUSING THE RUN OF LIFE
8/25/88 BASKETED IN STAVING
8/26/88 BATTLEMENTS TURNED TOWARDS THE DAY
8/29/88 PAUSING THROUGH THE WORD OF DAY
8/30/88 THE STORY OF THE MASSIVE DREAMS

9/1/88 UNSUSPECTED PANIC HERE
9/2/88 POINTS TO PLACEMENT FORMING
9/6/88 A SICKNESS, DEATH TO TIME
9/7/88 WITHIN THE AFTER, PAST THE NOON
9/8/88 AND SPEAKING NOT THE SEEN
9/9/88 STRANGE WITHIN THE CONTACT SPACE
9/10/88 WRONG AFTERNOON ENCHAINED
9/13/88 TO BE SO DAMNED AGAIN
9/14/88 THE DEATHLY MODES OF HATE
9/15/88 IN BLASTED NIGHT ALONE
9/16/88 FAR TOO BUSY TO MOVE OR THINK
9/17/88 IN CHURNING TIME APPROACHING GONE
9/22/88 IMAGE PARTING, SO LONG HELD
9/23/88 AMID THE MOTION CLAD OF TIME
9/24/88 THE UNEXPECTED COME AGAIN
9/25/88 WITHIN THE DARK, THE MOTION, SPACE
9/26/88 BAD PLACE WORSE WITHIN
9/27/88 THE PLACE IS NOT THE PAIN
9/28/88 DIRECTIONS AMID THE DAY
9/29/88 TRIPARTITION OF ALL THINGS SAID
9/30/88 BATHED IN FOULEST LIFE

10/3/88 DRAINING TOWARDS THE BLACK
10/4/88 AS LOWER PLACES, THESE
10/5/88 THAT SUICIDE MAKE FREE FROM HELL
10/6/88 DASHED AND HAZY, SO PERPLEXED
10/7/88 WRONGLY FOUND AMID RIGHT TIME
10/10/88 THIS FORMED FROM ACHING DARK
10/11/88 SWEPT UP WITHIN THAT RUSHING TIDE
10/12/88 POLARITY'S REPULSION, PAIN
10/13/88 AS PLACED WITHIN THE CHRONIC STREAM
10/14/88 THE WAY TO FORMING SIGHT
10/15/88 APART, ALONE, AWAITING
10/16/88 IN WASTED STATES FORLORN
10/17/88 OUT THROUGH THOSE REALMS OF SIGHT
10/18/88 ALWAYS, ALWAYS, ALWAYS RAGE
10/19/88 A GOODNESS NEVER QUITE ATTAINED
10/20/88 SOMETIME SOME WAYS
10/21/88 THE FROZEN FLOW OF DEATH
10/24/88 PART OF THESE DECAYS
10/25/88 FORMING PER THE LIGHT DESIGNED
10/26/88 FINAL SANDS WE TENSE AWAIT
10/29/88 WOODED, DISTANT, NOT QUITE RIGHT

11/1/88 FROM HEAVEN INTO HELL
11/2/88 IN BECOMING THE DANCE
11/3/88 IN UNCLEAR SIGHT AND OTHER SIDES DIVINING
11/4/88 IN HOPE DROWNED BY OUR FEARS
11/5/88 CRUSHED VOID OF AFTERNOONS
11/7/88 TO HURT, TO DIE, TO KILL
11/8/88 NAMED AGAINST THE TIME IN PAIN
11/9/88 THE TRACINGS OF SOME TORTURED TOME
11/10/88 WHERE NOT TO BE WHERE IS
11/11/88 TEMPORAL PLACE AGAINST THE NIGHT
11/14/88 TO NAME THAT FUTURE DAY
11/15/88 OF STORMS AMONGST THE STORM
11/16/88 DISJOINTED, SET OFF FROM THE WORLD
11/17/88 A SUDDEN BURSTING INTO FLAME
11/18/88 DIVISIVE NUMBERS SET IN WAIT
11/21/88 CAUGHT AGAIN, DRAGGED DOWN
11/22/88 A NERVOUSNESS, A FEAR WITHIN
11/23/88 CAUSED TO BE IN DIVISION
11/26/88 THE FORMING OF TRANSMISSION
11/28/88 ARISING TO RETURN THE CURSE
11/29/88 BADE BY MASSED DELAY

12/1/88 ALL HELL HERE FOUND IN DAY
12/2/88 THE CITY AND ITS GRIP
12/5/88 THE ILLNESS TAKING LEAVE
12/6/88 NOW BLOCKED OUT INTO TIME
12/7/88 OF WHAT NOT ME IS ME
12/8/88 POSITIONS IN THE TIDE
12/9/88 AGAINST THE PEOPLE OF THE DAY
12/12/88 INSUFFICIENCE, WHOLE UNTIED
12/13/88 DISLOCATED, BUFFETED BY DAY
12/14/88 ANNIHILATION'S PRAYER
12/15/88 TO FIND IN CHAOS CALM
12/16/88 THE NEXUS, FOCUS, CROSS-HAIR LINE
12/19/88 DESCENT ARISES TO DESCRY
12/20/88 A WAIT FOR TIME AWAITING
12/21/88 WHO COMES TO KILL UNANSWERED?
12/22/88 'TIS THE SEASON TO BE HATEFUL
12/23/88 LOST AMID THE BARRIERS
12/26/88 BROKEN PROMISE, SHATTERED DAY
12/27/88 A BALANCE FRAGILE KEPT
12/28/88 A FLIGHT INTO NEW CHANGE

www.ingramcontent.com/pod-product-compliance
Lightning Source LLC
Chambersburg PA
CBHW081915180426
43198CB00038B/2641